Leather
Decoration

Leather Decoration

BY HERB GENFAN
AND
LYN TAETZSCH

WATSON-GUPTILL PUBLICATIONS/NEW YORK

PITMAN PUBLISHING/LONDON

Copyright © 1975 by Watson-Guptill Publications

First published 1975 in the United States and Canada by Watson-Guptill Publications,
a division of Billboard Publications, Inc.,
One Astor Plaza, New York, N.Y. 10036

Library of Congress Cataloging in Publication Data
Taetzsch, Lyn.
  Leather decoration.
  Includes index.
  1. Leather work. I. Genfan, Herb, joint author.
II. Title.
TT290.T3   745.53′1   74–32390
ISBN 0–8230–2710–4

Published in Great Britain by Sir Isaac Pitman & Sons Ltd.,
39 Parker Street, London WC2B 5PB
ISBN 0–273–00908–7

Manufactured in U.S.A.

First Printing, 1975

To our parents,
and our children—
Vicki, Blixy, and Mark.

Contents

ACKNOWLEDGMENTS

We thank all of our editors at Watson-Guptill for their help in this and all our books. We thank all of the leather craftspeople who have contributed photographs of their work to this book, and especially the employees of Holy Cow Leather, whose work went into many of the projects shown. We thank Mary and Braum Azerbegi of Braum's Leather in Berkeley, California, for being our first tutors in leathercraft and starting us on our way.

The appliqué on this cape was drawn freehand, cut out and glued to the cape one layer at a time, then stitched down with a sewing maching. By Lassie Rathbone. Photograph by Eric Borg.

Introduction

In this book, we've compiled a number of modern techniques for decorating leather. Our idea of decoration covers a broad range of effects: coloring, drawing, texturing, appliqué, stitching and lacing, riveting, and adding hardware. These methods can be used on many kinds of projects and with a variety of leathers. Naturally, some techniques are better suited to certain projects and types of leather than others, so, in each chapter, we've indicated which leathers are best for that particular technique. And, the photo gallery of finished projects at the end of each chapter illustrates some of the many possible articles that can be decorated using that technique.

You may notice that some of the projects combine several decorative techniques. For instance, tooling, stamping, and carving are enhanced by shading or dyeing of the leather. Since you'll probably want to combine two or more methods in your work also, we suggest that you skim the whole book, then practice individual techniques on scrap leather. Once you've mastered these, try pairing methods together on more scrap leather. Finally, after enough experimentation, you'll be able to choose from all the processes to achieve exactly the effects you're looking for in a specific project.

1

Shading

Shading is the process of dyeing a piece of leather so that it's dark on the perimeter and gradually becomes lighter toward the center of the leather, until the dye blends with the natural color of the leather. This brings out all the grain, markings, and other textures, giving the piece of leather a rich, modeled look. Shading should be done after all pieces of a project are cut, holes punched, etc., but *before* the pieces are sewn, laced, or riveted. The process adds depth and beauty to any finished piece, whether it's a handbag, a belt, or even a very small item such as a keyring. Once you've mastered shading, you'll want to use it in combination with many of the decorative techniques in this book, such as stamping and leather-burning.

MATERIALS

1. Leather dye (alcohol base).
2. Dye rag (this can be any soft, absorbent piece of material, such as terrycloth).
3. Wool or felt dauber.
4. Saddle soap.
5. Sheepskin scraps.
6. Harness dressing.
7. A small sponge.

Generally, an unfinished leather, such as latigo cowhide, will work best. Other than that, you can experiment with any light-colored leather, as long as it doesn't have a suede finish. If the leather is a very light beige, a tan or light brown dye will be best for shading. The darker the original leather color, the darker the dye should be.

PROBLEMS

If dye drips onto the surface of the leather while you're dyeing the edge with the dauber, you're applying too much pressure, or else your dauber has too much dye on it. Be sure to scrape the dauber against the lip of the bottle top as you pull it out, in order to remove excess dye.

If your dyeing rag becomes worn or develops ridges of folded material, streaking and other uneven shading effects may result. Keep your dyeing rag smooth at all times; if it wears through in one spot, refold it or take a new rag.

Another problem that may occur, especially when shading a very small piece of leather, is too much dye on the rag. When this happens, you'll find yourself quickly covering the whole piece, or making too abrupt a transition from dark to light areas. To remove excess dye, pat the dye rag on a scrap of leather or newspaper before you apply it to the leather.

Step 1. *First, dye the edges of the leather, using a dauber. Dip the dauber into a bottle of dye and squeeze out the excess as you take the dauber from the bottle. With a continuous, steady movement, cover the entire edge of the leather. If the dauber begins to skip, redip it in the bottle of dye.*

Step 2. *Next, cut or tear a piece of cloth about 4" x 8". Fold it twice. Holding the folded cloth over the top of the dye bottle, quickly turn the bottle upside down. Remove excess dye from the cloth by scraping the rag on the lip of the bottle.*

Step 3. *Starting at the perimeter of the leather, rub carefully in light strokes.*

Step 4. *Gradually move inward toward the center of the leather, using a lighter and lighter touch. As the dyeing rag becomes drier, you should exert more pressure. The object is to have the dye color melt gradually into the natural leather color. Depending on the size of the piece and the amount of shading desired, this process may be repeated one or more times until the proper effect is reached.*

Step 5. *Once the leather has been shaded, saddle soap should be rubbed into it to give it a finished look. Rub a sheepskin scrap into a can of saddle soap, then rub the scrap hard on the edges of the leather. This will smooth down the rough fibers, making an attractive modeled curve.*

Step 6. *When the edges have been thoroughly soaped and rubbed, lay the leather flat and apply soap to the surface. Rub it in well, using ample elbow grease.*

Step 7. *If a finer, shinier finish is desired, a light coat of harness dressing may be added. Wet a small sponge and wring it out until almost dry. Moisten the sponge with harness dressing, and with light, circular strokes, cover the surface of the leather.*

Step 8. *Let the leather dry for two or three minutes before you touch it.*

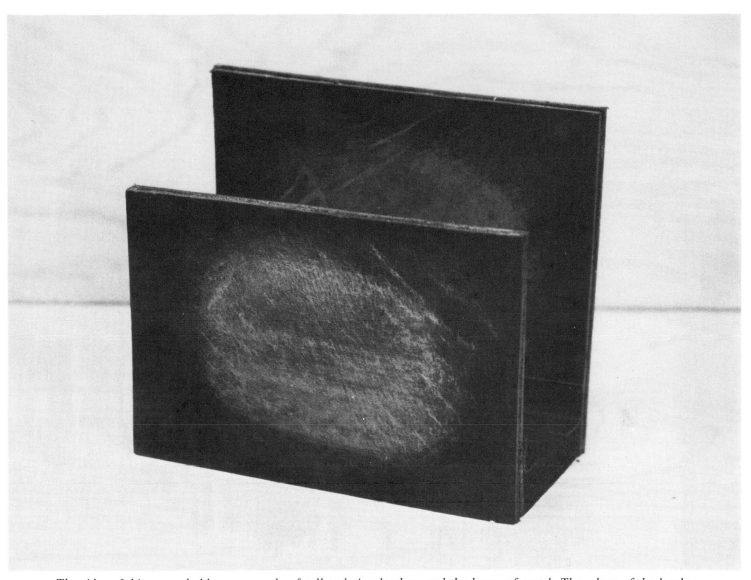

The sides of this paper holder were made of yellow latigo leather, and the base, of wood. The edges of the leather were shaded a dark brown and gradually blended into the surface of the leather. By Holy Cow Leather.

Made of 2–2 1/2 oz. kip, this billfold was stamped, then dyed, saddle soaped, and finished with harness dressing. By Holy Cow Leather.

The bottom of this handbag is calico-flesh cowhide, and the top is latigo which was decorated with awl lines, stamped, and shaded with dye around the edges. The bag has a snap closing and a removable shoulder strap, also of latigo. By Holy Cow Leather.

2

Dyeing

Many leathers, such as suede and glove leather, are dyed various colors at the tannery. These leathers are saturated with the color, and are designed to be used without further dyeing. The dye process we're talking about in this book will color only the surface of the leather, but it will be a permanent, non-bleeding finish.

Leather dye comes in a full range of colors, and you can mix them to obtain even more shades. You can achieve such effects as a flat, overall color, stripes, or mottling. After tooling, carving, stamping, and awl drawing, dyeing the piece of leather will bring out the design more clearly and effectively. Dyeing should also be done after all pieces of a project are cut, holes punched, etc., but *before* the pieces are sewn, laced, or riveted.

MATERIALS

1. Leather dye (alcohol base).
2. Dye rag.
3. A wool or felt dauber.

If you want to dye the leather light colors, start with a light, neutral leather. Natural kip, live oak tooling leather, neutral latigo, and shoulders should work satisfactorily. The darker the original color of the leather, the darker and muddier the dye will look on it. A very yellow leather will make blue dye look green, although it will produce richer shades of brown. Experiment on small scraps before choosing the leather and dye color combination.

PROBLEMS

If your piece of leather ends up with a dark blotch marring the overall color, you may have held your hand too long in that spot. Or, you may have had too much dye on your rag and started on that spot. Be sure to move your hand quickly over the whole area, *gradually* achieving the color depth desired.

If, when dyeing a piece that has been tooled, stamped, or carved, you find that the design fills up with dye, you probably have too much dye on your rag, or are pressing too hard. Don't start dyeing right over the design area, but, instead, work gradually towards it with a light touch.

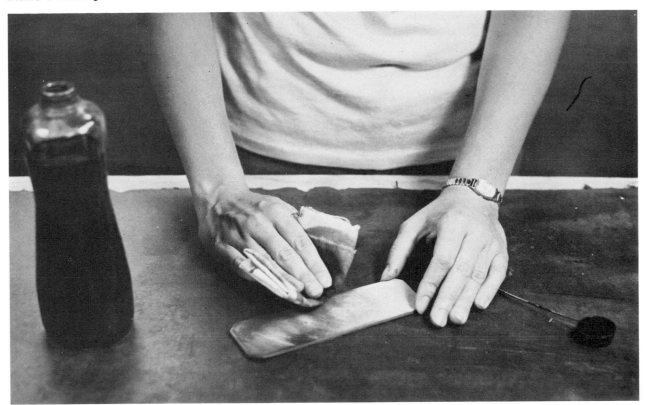

Step 1. *After you have dyed the edges of the leather with a dauber (as described in Chapter 1), go over the surface of the leather with a dye-moistened rag, using light, circular strokes. Work from one end of the leather to the other, covering the whole surface.*

Step 2. *When the rag becomes dry, rewet it and go over the whole area again and again until all the pores are filled with an even, solid color. Keep your hand moving at all times, because if you rest it on one spot, it will leave a darker area which will show up against the rest of the surface.*

Step 1. *To achieve stripes, use a dauber instead of a rag for dyeing. Making sure your dauber is fairly filled with dye, start at the left-hand bottom edge of the leather.*

Step 2. *Sweep the dauber across the leather in a straight, even line.*

Step 3. *Refilling the dauber with dye, begin again on the left-hand edge of the leather, about 1/2″ up from the bottom, so that this stroke slightly overlaps the previous one. With a steady hand, glide the dauber evenly across the piece of leather.*

Step 4. *Repeat this process, moving up another 1/2″ or so each time, until the entire piece of leather has been covered. Wherever the dauber overlapped, a darker line of color will be left. This effect is especially nice on belts.*

Step 1. *To achieve a mottled effect, touch the leather all over with a dauber, leaving dyed spots of various sizes.*

Step 2. *Take a slightly damp dyeing rag and lightly go over the whole surface. The original spotting will appear darker than the overall color, producing a mottled or spotted effect.*

Step 1. *Use care when dyeing a piece of leather which has been tooled, carved, stamped, etc. First wipe the excess dye from your dye rag.*

Step 2. *Start with very light strokes, especially over the design. As your rag becomes drier you can rub harder, bringing the design into sharper focus.*

Step 3. *When you've finished dyeing the pieces of leather for a project, saddle soap and finish them as described in Chapter 1.*

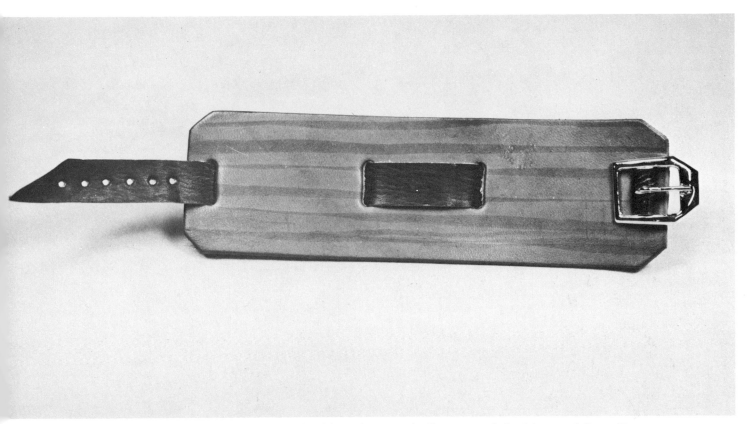

This watchband was made of 6/7 oz. russet shoulder. The striped effect was acheived by carefully pulling a dauber full of dye across the leather, overlapping it slightly each time. By Lyn Taetzsch.

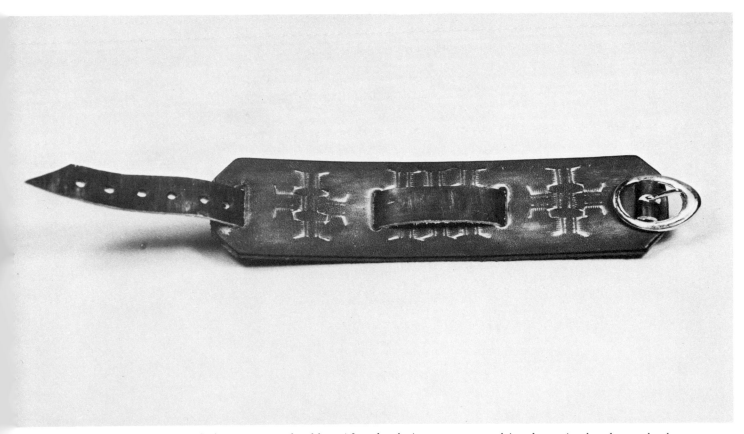

This watchband is made of 6/7 oz. russet shoulder. After the design was stamped in, the entire band was dyed. By Holy Cow Leather.

First, the lines on this 1 3/4" belt were drawn with an awl, then the circles were stamped in with a round stamping tool. Finally, the belt was shaded with leather dye, which brought out the line design. By Lyn Taetzsch.

Note the interesting dyeing effects on these handbags. After the design was stamped in, a coat of Fiebings Antique Dye was applied to the surface and allowed to dry. Then, a dark brown antique finish was applied and rubbed into the stamping impressions, and wiped off the surface with a rag, leaving the impressions darker than the rest of the bag. The closings were made with the tips of deer antlers, which were sanded down and oiled with lemon oil. By Mary Phelps of Scorpio Leather, East Orleans, Massachuseits.

3

Painting with Dye

Dyeing with a paintbrush provides the additional control necessary for detail and varied expression. Nonobjective, abstract, or realistic painting can be achieved on leather as well as on canvas or paper. The process consists simply of dipping a paintbrush into dye and applying it to the leather. Various brush sizes and strokes can produce many different effects, from pinpoints to broad areas of color. A fine-tipped paintbrush can be used to fill in the design areas with different colors before dyeing the whole piece.

Dye, like paint, can be mixed to achieve various shades and colors. Blue and yellow will make green, red and yellow will make orange, etc. You may find some difficulty, however, when mixing white with other colors. You can't dye a brown or tan leather white with a standard alcohol-based dye. The color of the leather will show through. Therefore, when you mix white with other colors in an attempt to achieve pastel shades, you may get an uneven, powdery result.

We add Fiebings Antique Finish to white dye in order to achieve pastel shades. Pink is made by mixing Oxblood Antique Finish with white dye and light blue is made by mixing Purple Antique Finish with white dye. It takes a bit of experimenting to come up with the proper combinations and quantities. These mixtures must be shaken thoroughly each time before using.

As with shading or dyeing, painting should be done after all pieces of a project are cut, holes punched, etc., but *before* the pieces are sewn, laced, or riveted. You may wish to trace or draw the picture or design onto the leather first with an awl or tracing tool.

MATERIALS

1. Leather dye (alcohol base).
2. Watercolor brushes of various sizes.
3. Soap.
4. Water.

In order to achieve the brightest, purest colors, you should use a pale, neutral-colored leather, such as natural kip, live oak tooling leather, neutral latigo, or shoulders.

PROBLEMS

If your colors come out dull and brownish, the leather you're painting is too dark. If your colors all come out with a yellowish tint, the leather is too yellow to begin with.

If, when painting a stamped design, the dye runs over the design onto the leather, you have too much dye on your brush or are using too large a brush. Always shake excess dye off into the bottle first.

If an application of white dye mixture comes out powdery and rubs off, you may have mixed in some of the sediment from the bottom of the white dye bottle. This mixture will have to be thrown away. Start again without shaking the white dye bottle and using only the top liquid.

Step 1. *Dip your brush into the dye. Shake off excess dye so the brush doesn't drip.*

Step 2. *With a light touch, apply the color in a few, even strokes. Pull the brush across the leather smoothly, covering as much of the desired area as possible with each stroke.*

Step 3. Use small brushes for the fine areas and wider brushes for the large areas.

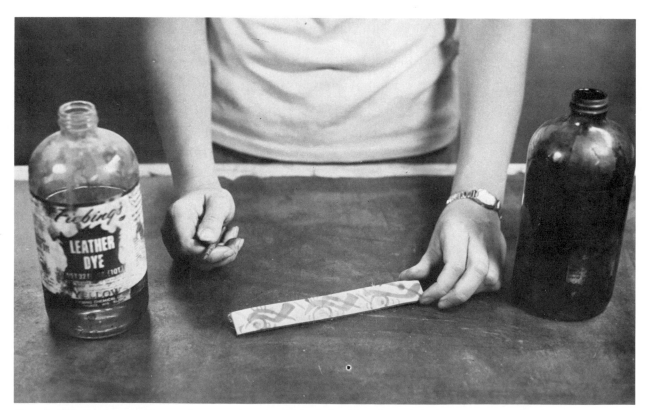

Step 4. Wherever a stroke overlaps another, you'll be left with a line of darker color, so take this into consideration when planning your design. Clean your brush with soap and water before using it for another color.

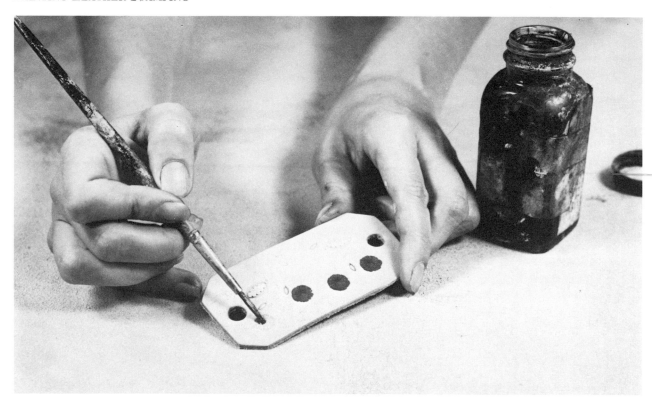

Step 1. *Completely fill each design with dye, using a pointed paintbrush to reach into the small indentations. If you plan to dye the whole piece of leather an overall light color, and the individual stamped designs a dark color, then you must paint the designs very carefully, or else the colors will show through. Of course, if you plan to dye the whole piece of leather an overall dark color, then you can put more dye on your brush and not worry about running over the outline.*

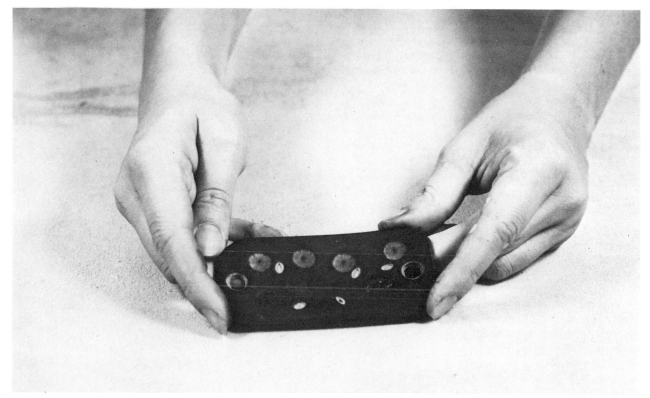

Step 2. *When you've finished painting, dye the surface of the leather with a dye rag. Then apply saddle soap and harness dressing as described in Chapter 1.*

The stippled effect on this box, made of leather and plywood, was achieved by spatter-painting the leather with different colors of dye. By Rosa Lee Davenport, Ithaca, New York.

The leaf design on this belt was made with stamping tools and painted a light green. Then the rest of the belt was dyed brown. Note the solid brass buckle. The belt is 8/9 oz. yellow latigo. By Mary Azerbegi, Berkeley, California.

The mushroom design on this wallet was first drawn with an awl, then shaded with dye and brush. Finally, the edges of the whole piece of leather were shaded with a dye rag. By Holy Cow Leather.

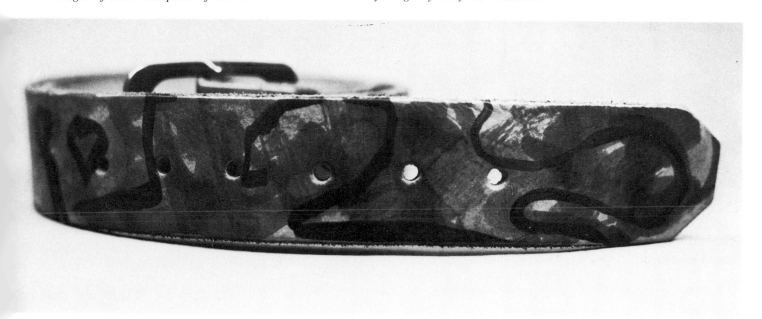

Paintbrushes and different colors of dye were used to create the design on this belt. By Lyn Taetzsch.

4

Painting with Acrylics

The *process* of painting leather with acrylic paint is similar to that of painting with dye, but the *effect* is much different. Both mediums are applied to the leather with a paintbrush, and with both, you can use various brush sizes, strokes, and shades of "paint." However, leather dye soaks into the leather, creating a muted, subtle coloring, while acrylics stay on the surface of the leather, retaining a hard, bright look. Acrylic paints can be mixed as you would poster paint: add white for light tints, black for darker values, and both white and black for grayed colors. Very subtle shading and coloring effects can be achieved in this manner.

Painting with acrylics (as with dyeing and shading) should be done after all pieces of a project are cut, holes punched, etc., but *before* the pieces are sewn, laced, or riveted. You may also wish to trace or draw the design on the leather first with an awl or tracing tool.

MATERIALS

1. Water-based acrylic paint.
2. Watercolor brushes of various sizes.
3. Soap.
4. Water.

Since the acrylics will sit on the surface of the leather and retain their opaque color, it's not as important to use a light-colored leather as it is when painting with dye. The only unsuitable leathers would be suede, or a leather with a glazed finish, or any finish that resists the acrylic paint. Pliable thin leathers may be painted, but will have a tendency to crack when bent or folded. Use a heavy, stiff leather for best results.

PROBLEMS

If the color comes out runny or if the leather shows through it, the consistency of the paint is too thin.

If the color won't adhere to the surface, the leather probably has a glaze or other finish which won't accept paint. Try another kind of leather.

If cracking occurs, you may have applied the paint too heavily, or its consistency may be too thick. Acrylic paint, which has been applied to a piece of leather that's bent a lot (such as a belt), will have a tendency to crack also.

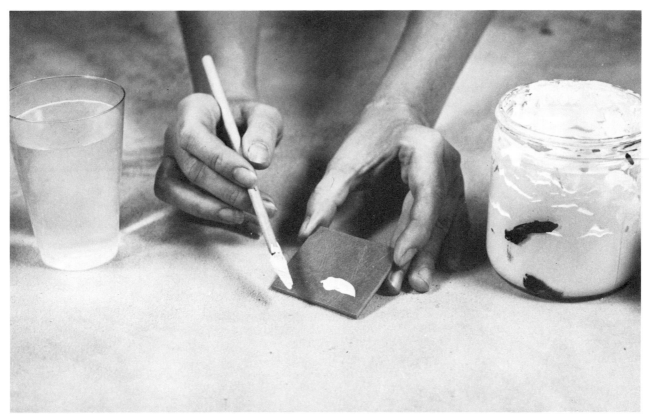

Step 1. First test the consistency of your paint. Add water, mix well, and try it out on a scrap of leather. The paint should be thick enough to cover the leather with an opaque, solid color, but not so heavy that it builds up thick blobs which may crack when dry.

Step 2. Paint with single, smooth strokes; try to cover an area with as few layers of paint as possible. The more layers you build up, the more likely the dried paint will crack later.

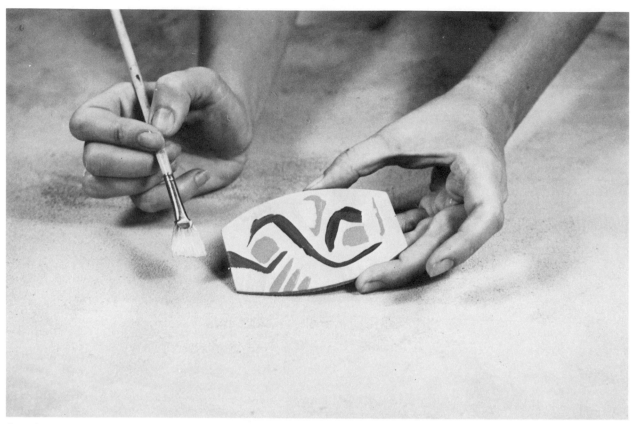

Step 3. *Use a new brush for each color, or else clean your brush thoroughly with soap and water before dipping it in a new color. A wide brush is best for wide strokes.*

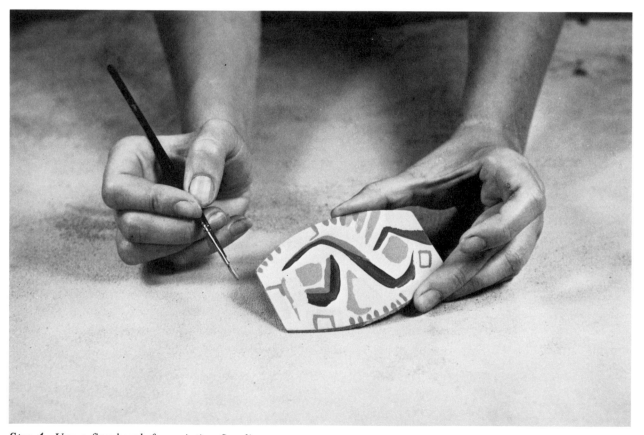

Step 4. *Use a fine brush for painting fine lines.*

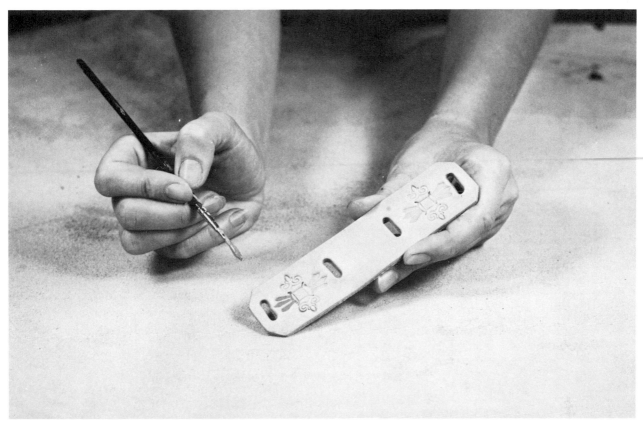

Step 5. *For painting in a stamped design, use a pointed brush, filling in each recessed area completely. Do a neat, accurate job because acrylics will show through the darkest dye.*

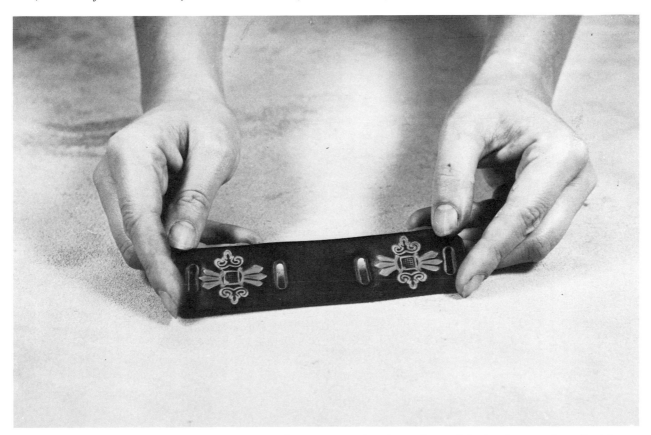

Step 6. *When the paint is thoroughly dry, use a dyeing rag to dye the surface of the leather, as described in Chapter 2. You may also wish to finish the leather, demonstrated in Chapter 1.*

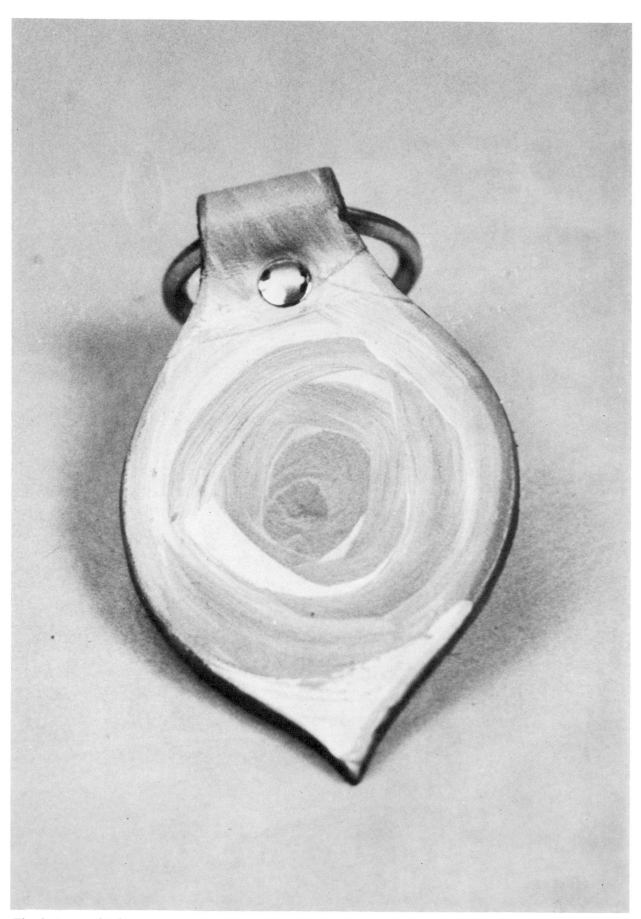

The design on this keyring was painted in acrylics. By Lyn Taetzsch.

The surface of this latigo belt was painted with acrylics to achieve the abstract design. By Lyn Taetzsch.

The design on this belt, made of 7/8 oz. latigo, was painted with acrylics. By Lyn Taetzsch.

5

Pen and Ink

Pen and ink technique provides fine-line, detailed effects. Almost any type of ink—drawing, fountain pen, ballpoint—can be used on leather, and an ink that's permanent on paper will also be permanent on leather. The ink is applied to the leather with a pen (stick, brush, or Magic Marker), and is absorbed quickly. By varying the penpoint or tool used, different effects can be achieved, from thick, heavy strokes to thin, sharp lines. Children, especially, will enjoy the freedom and ease of decorating leather with Magic Markers or ballpoint pens. Be sure you don't use water-soluble markers—use, instead, those that are made with permanent inks. To test ballpoint pen ink for permanency, draw on some scrap leather, and then rub the inked lines hard to see if they smear.

Inking can also be combined with other methods—dyeing, shading, painting—to provide an infinite variety of possible results. For example, you may wish to use pen and ink to sketch in a design before painting, or to highlight a design after painting. Inking can be done either before or after the leather has been shaded with dye, but should always be done *after* all pieces of a project are cut, holes punched, etc., and *before* the pieces are sewn, laced, or riveted.

MATERIALS

1. Ink (waterproof is best for permanency).
2. Penholder.
3. A set of penpoints in a variety of widths.
4. Your choice of bamboo pens, sharpened sticks, paintbrushes.

You can use pen and ink on just about any kind of leather, however if it has a highly glazed finish, the leather may resist the ink.

PROBLEMS

If large ink blots occur when you place your pen on the leather, you probably have too much ink on the penpoint. Shake or wipe off excess ink before starting.

If the ink lines smear during saddle soaping, you haven't waited long enough for them to dry. Or, you may be using a nonpermanent ink. Test all ink on scrap pieces of leather first.

If you have difficulty controlling your pen lines, draw your design lightly first with an awl. Begin with light penstrokes, becoming bolder and darker as you become sure of the final results you're seeking.

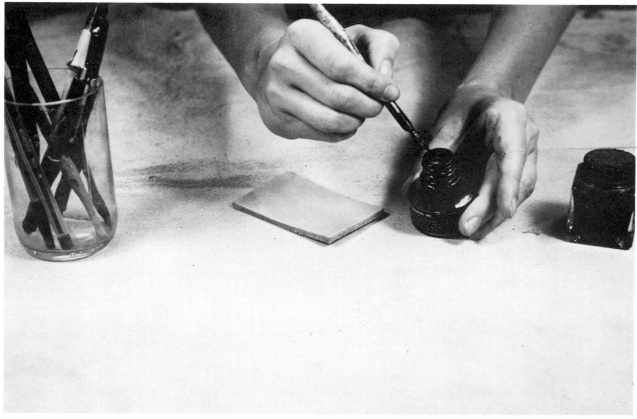

Step 1. *First practice ink strokes on a piece of scrap leather. After dipping your pen into the ink, wipe the pen against the rim of the jar to remove excess ink.*

Step 2. *Draw the pen smoothly and evenly across the leather, moving slowly enough that the pen doesn't skip, but quickly enough that the ink doesn't seep too deeply into the leather and create a blot.*

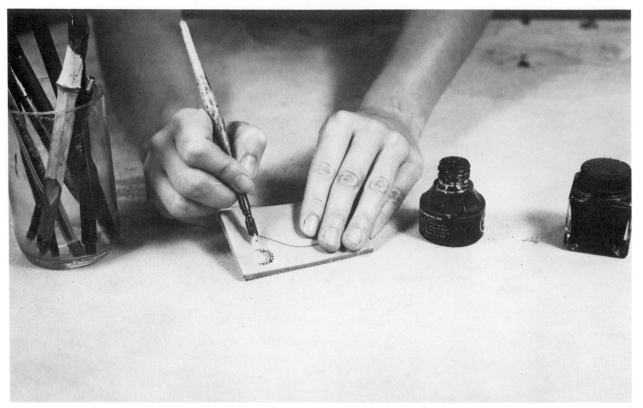

Step 3. *To achieve stippled effects, touch the penpoint to the leather quickly; each touch will leave a dot. These dots, when repeated close together, give the illusion of shading. With different penpoints—round, square, flat—you can make a variety of stippled effects.*

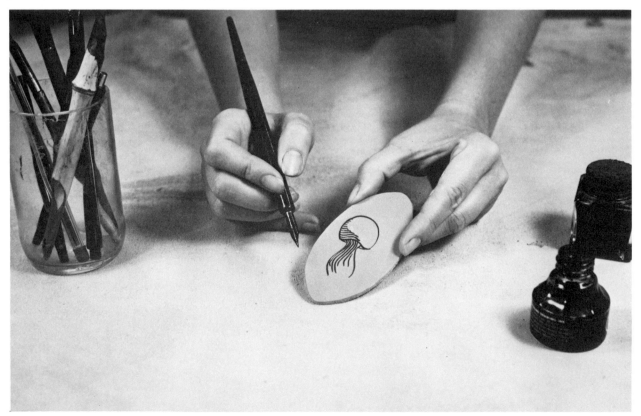

Step 4. *Thin lines, placed closely together, can also be used to create shadows and three-dimensional effects. With a very fine penpoint, carefully draw each line next to the previous one, varying the distance between lines to create movement in the piece.*

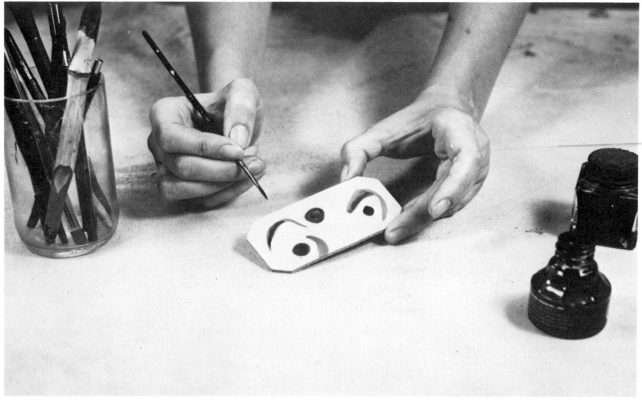

Step 1. *Use a paintbrush with ink just as you would use it with dye.*

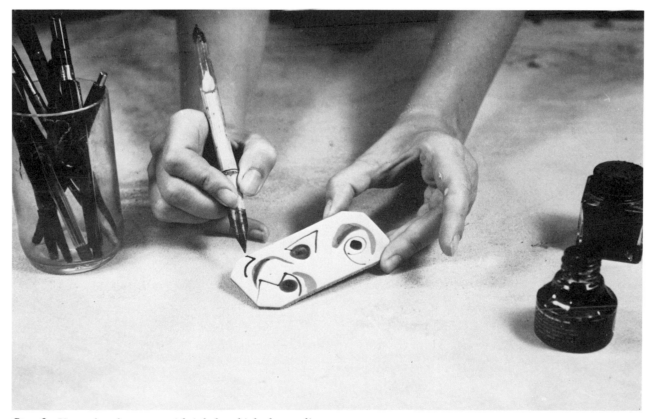

Step 2. *Use a bamboo pen with ink for thick, heavy lines.*

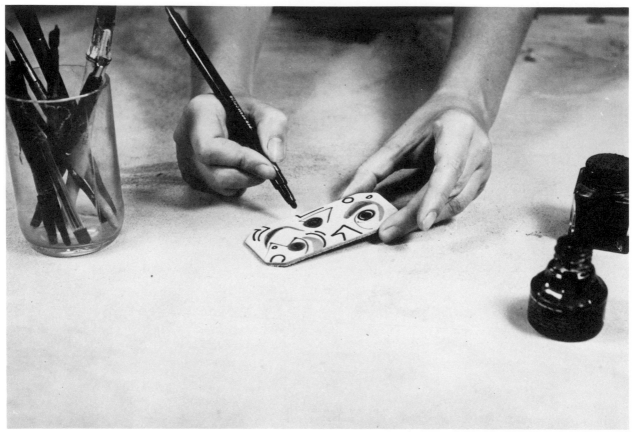

Step 3. *Magic Markers work fine on leather; always use those that have permanent inks.*

Step 4. *Non-smearing ballpoint pens can also be used on leather.*

The design on this keyring was done with a Magic Marker. By Lyn Taetzsch.

These keyrings illustrate how children enjoy using Magic Markers (above) and ballpoint pens (right) to draw on leather.

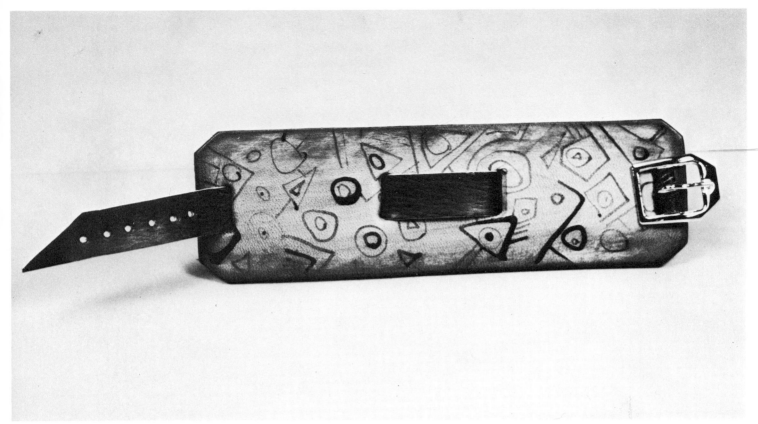

The design on this watchband was drawn with various pens and inks. The edges of the band were shaded slightly with leather dye. By Lyn Taetzsch.

6

Stamping

Leather stamping is one of the most popular methods of decorating leather today. Besides the traditional stamping tools in geometric, flower, leaf, and other designs, today you can purchase stamping tools in American Indian, Art Nouveau, Victorian, and other innovative subjects. Leather stamping is accomplished by holding a stamping tool against a piece of leather and hitting the tool with a mallet. The steel stamping tool impresses a design into soft leather. Once the design is impressed deeply enough, it will remain in the leather.

Stamping should be done after all pieces of a project are cut, holes punched, etc., but before the pieces are dyed, sewn, laced, or riveted. Stamping can be done using just a worktable for a base, but it's much easier and more effectively accomplished by placing the leather on a wood block, tree stump, or a 1″ to 2″ thick steel plate. We use a steel plate 2″ thick by 10″ wide by 20″ long. If you don't use a plate or block, you'll have to hit the stamping tool harder and/or more times to make an impression.

The best approach to leather stamping is to first plan your design and choose the tools you need to execute it. Then, before you stamp your design on the actual project, it's a good idea to test it on a piece of scrap leather. We like to spend a couple of hours every now and then just fooling around with the tools on scrap leather. Then we pick out the best of these designs to use on future projects.

MATERIALS

1. Rawhide mallet (try a 2″ and a 3″ head to see which suits you best).
2. A chopping block, tree stump, or a 1–2″ thick steel plate.
3. Your choice of stamping tools.

We have found latigo of all weights from 3–4 oz. and up to be excellent for stamping. We also stamp 2–2½ oz. kip, although this requires some care because it's so thin. There are leathers made specially for stamping, such as Tandy's Nature-Tand leather. Tell your leather supplier what you're going to do with the leather and he'll recommend the best type.

PROBLEMS

If you find it difficult to hit the mallet squarely on the head of the stamping tool, it could be that your mallet has worn down in the center. You can either replace the mallet or saw off ¼″, leaving a flat, smooth surface again.

If the stamping tool makes a hole in the leather, you may be using leather which is too thin. Or, you may have hit a soft, weak spot in that particular piece. Remember—a piece of leather isn't uniform in thickness and consistency like a piece of plastic. Watch out for soft or thin areas when cutting out your project.

Step 1. *Place the leather on the block or steel plate. Hold the stamping tool firmly, with your thumb on one side and four fingers on the other. (If you're right-handed, hold the tool in your left hand, and vice versa.)*

Step 2. *Grip the mallet firmly in your other hand and hit the tool squarely on the head. At first you may be afraid that you'll hit your hand with the mallet. Practice hitting the tool lightly until you become confident enough to give it a good strong whack.*

Step 3. *Tools with sharp or small design areas will go more easily into the leather and therefore don't have to be hit as hard. If you do hit them too hard, they'll sink right through the leather and possibly make a hole in it. The trick is to hit each tool with exactly the proper strength to make a clear impression equal in depth to those made by all the other tools you're using.*

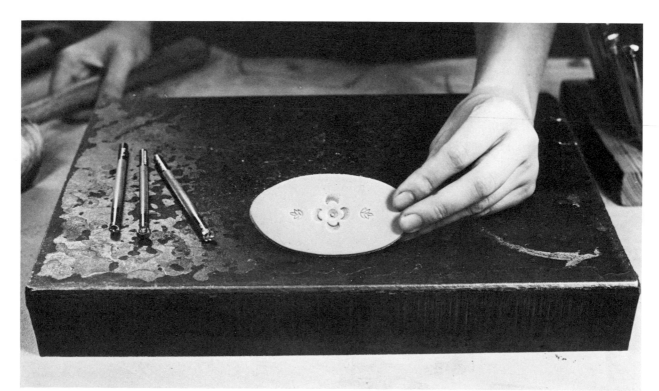

Step 4. *Some craftspeople prefer to wet the leather before stamping, which makes the leather more pliable and easier to stamp. They soak it in a pail of water for a few minutes, then lay it out on the block and begin stamping. Other craftspeople also prefer to tap each tool lightly many times with the mallet, rather than giving it one good shot. We find our method quicker, however, and just as accurate once control is obtained through experience. You can, of course, combine various stamping tools to achieve your design.*

Step 5. *Once you've stamped your design into the leather, you'll probably want to use one or more of the coloring methods described in Chapters 1 through 5. These will emphasize and enhance the stamped design. If you use our method of stamping, dyeing can be done immediately. If you wet the leather first, however, let it dry thoroughly before beginning to paint or dye it. Whether you dye, paint the leather, or leave it plain, it still should be saddle soaped and finished after stamping. See Chapter 1 for details.*

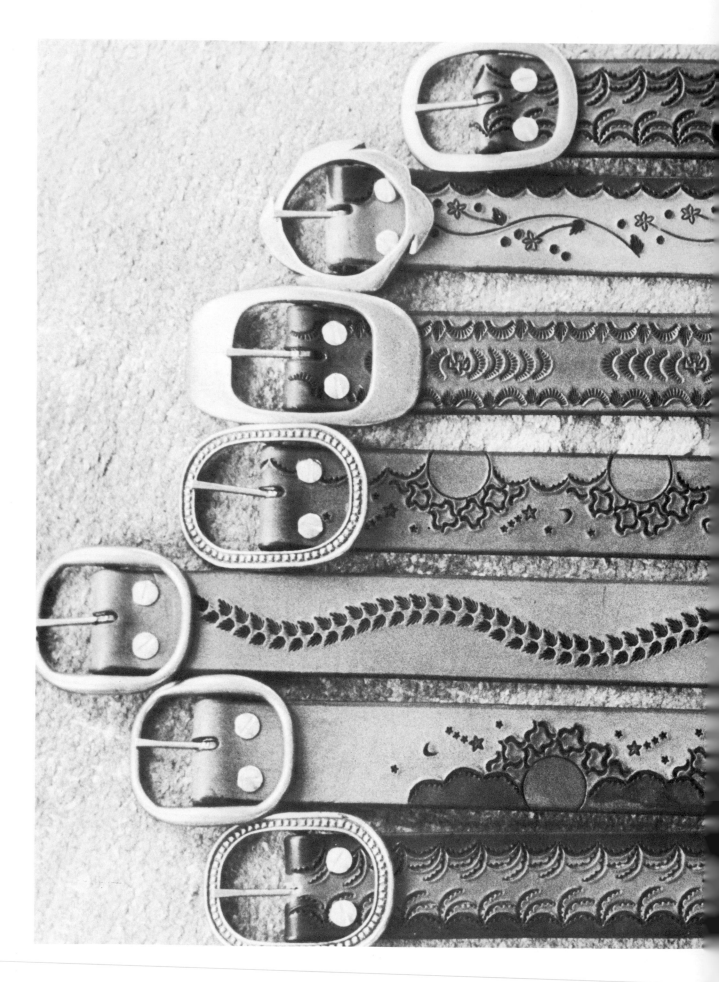

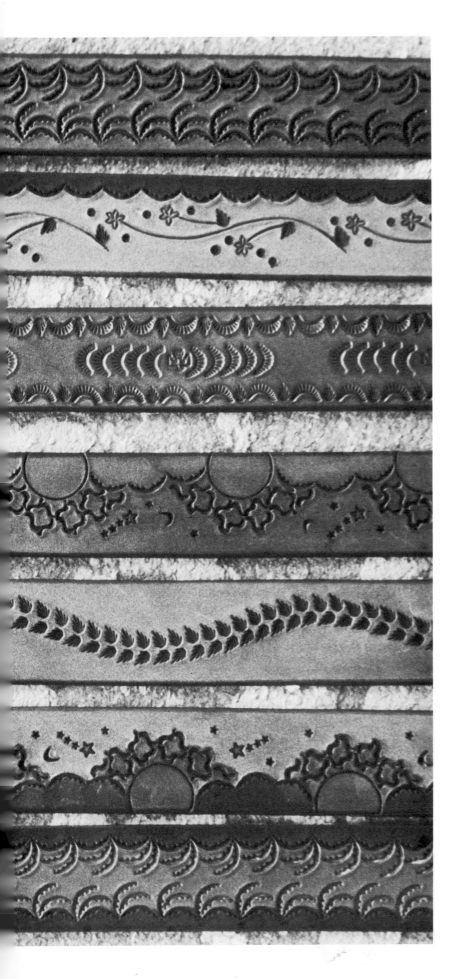

These leather belts are made from vegetable-tanned shoulder leather. Most of the designs were stamped in, although the lines were made with a ruby-tipped, swivel-blade knife. By Mary Phelps of Scorpio Leather, East Orleans, Massachusetts. Photograph by Gabriel Cooney.

This wallet was hand stamped, then shaded with dye. By Holy Cow Leather.

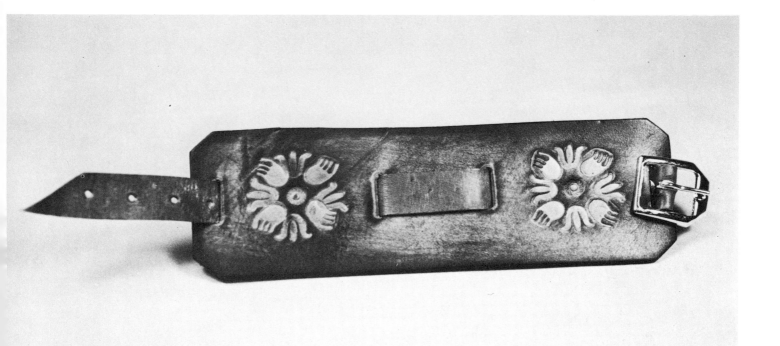

This watchband is made of 7/8 oz. yellow latigo. The design was produced with stamping tools, then the whole piece was dyed. By Holy Cow Leather.

The design on this watchband, made of 6/7 oz. russet shoulder, was made with stamping tools and brought out with brown dye. By Holy Cow Leather.

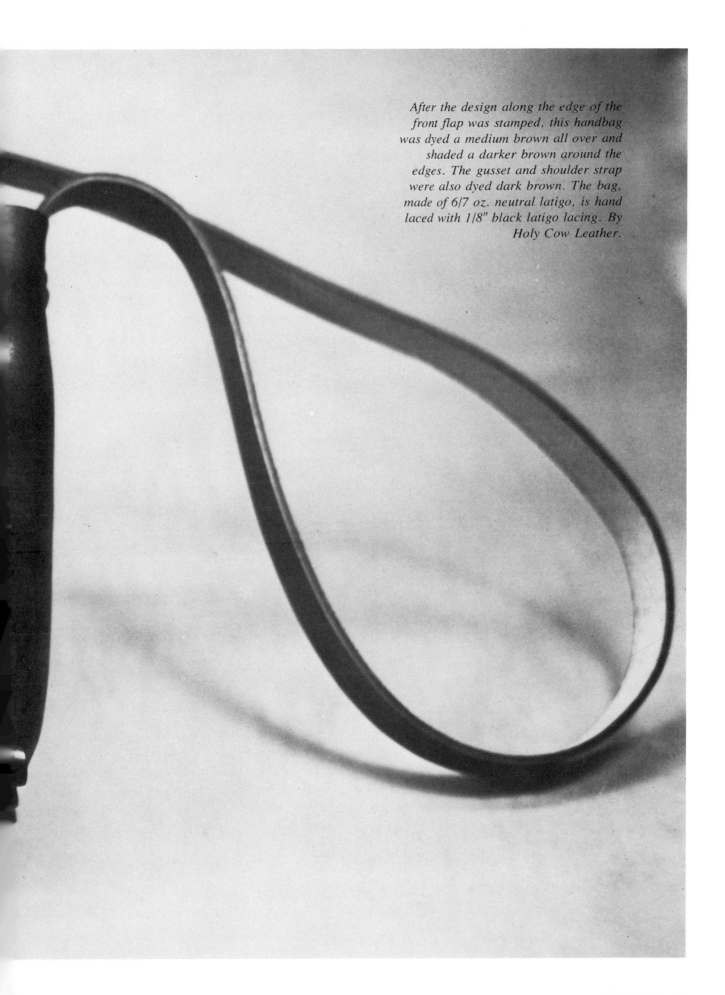

After the design along the edge of the front flap was stamped, this handbag was dyed a medium brown all over and shaded a darker brown around the edges. The gusset and shoulder strap were also dyed dark brown. The bag, made of 6/7 oz. neutral latigo, is hand laced with 1/8" black latigo lacing. By Holy Cow Leather.

7

Tooling

Leather tooling is an old form of leather decoration traditionally used to create intricate floral patterns so popular in the "Western" look. You can update this technique to create your own personal, original designs, or use it in combination with stamping and carving for a wider range of effects.

The technique of tooling consists of pressing or rubbing modeling tools of various shapes and sizes against the leather when it's wet. This forms depressions and textures which remain after the leather has dried. Areas which haven't been tooled stand out in relief against the tooled areas.

Tooling should be done after all pieces of a project are cut, holes punched, etc., but *before* the pieces are dyed, painted, sewn, laced, or riveted. Just as in stamping, it's a good idea to practice using the tools on scrap leather first. Experiment to discover the different effects each tool will produce. By varying the pressure on the tool (and the way you hold it), you'll be able to create depressions, lines, curves, and so forth.

MATERIALS

1. A set of modeling tools.
2. Some water.

There are many modeling tools specially made for beveling, depressing outlines, fine work, tracing patterns, etc. You may want to start out with a small kit of assorted tools. By experimenting, you can find which ones produce the sort of effects you're looking for. As far as leather goes, a vegetable-tanned leather is best, but latigo, shoulder, and other heavy cowhides will also work. Again, ask your leather supplier which of his leathers he recommends for tooling.

PROBLEMS

If you have difficulty getting the depth of impression you want, perhaps your leather isn't wet enough. You also may find it necessary to go over and over a particular area to get it just the way you want it.

If you find your design disappearing as the leather dries, you may need to switch to a different kind of leather, or you may not have made your original tooling deep enough.

Step 1. *Soak the leather thoroughly in a pail of water. If the leather dries out as you're working on it, resoak it.*

Step 2. *Plan your design and choose the tools you need. You may wish to trace the design from a piece of paper or pattern first. Use a pointed modeling tool to trace the design on the leather.*

Step 3. *Now decide which areas you want to stand out or be raised in the design, and which ones you want depressed. Start beveling the leather down away from the outline of the raised areas.*

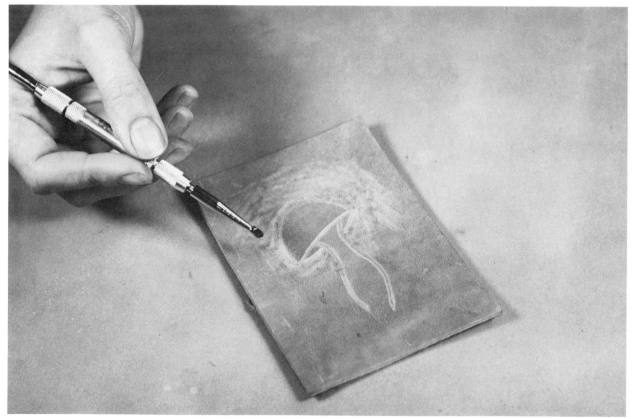

Step 4. *Use the flat-tipped tools for large, depressed areas.*

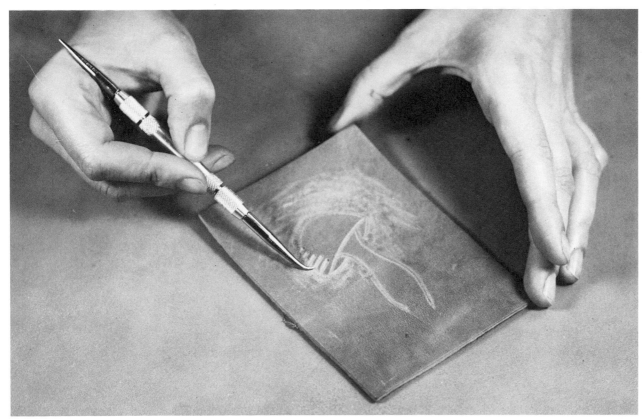

Step 5. *Use small, pointed tools for details.*

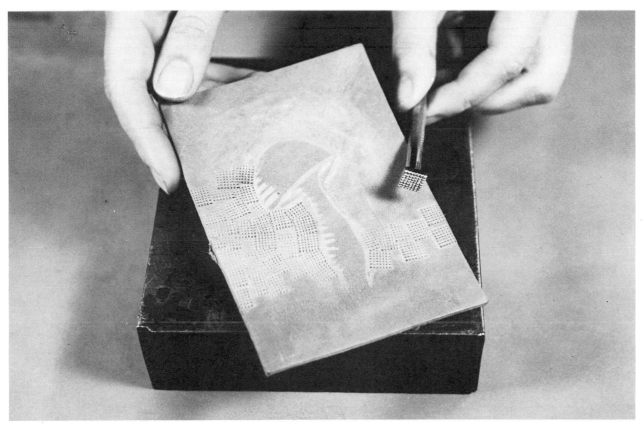

Step 6. *You may wish to use stamping tools to create texture in the background areas of your tooled designs. There are stamping tools created specifically for this purpose. Or you might use stamping tools within your design for special emphasis.*

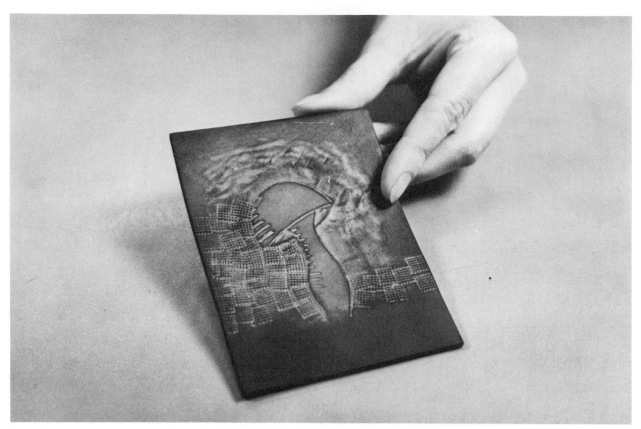

Step 7. *Let the piece of leather dry thoroughly before dyeing or saddle soaping. Since tooling creates a subtler effect than stamping, more care is required in dyeing or painting. A lot of the design could be lost by heavy dyeing techniques. We suggest lightly shading with a very dry rag, achieving the desired effects slowly and carefully. Or, you may wish to simply saddle soap and finish the piece without any further coloring (see Chapter 1 for details).*

The bulging effect of these handbags, made of vegetable-tanned shoulder leather, was achieved by shaping the leather while wet, using the round end of a tool. The edges of both bags were cobbled with solid brass clinching nails, and the texture of the bag on the right was acheived by pounding the leather with the butt end of a balpeen hammer.

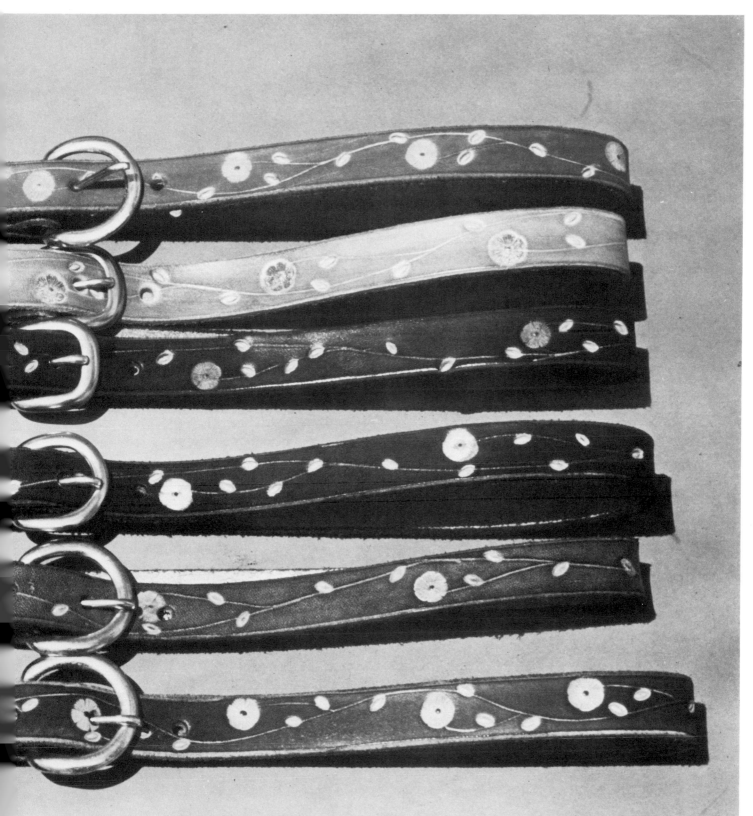

These belts are 3/4" wide and made of 6/7 oz. natural tooling leather. First the vines were drawn with an awl, and the flowers, seeds, and leaves made with stamping tools. Then the flowers and leaves were painted with brush and dye, and the belts were dyed overall solid colors. The buckles and keepers are gilt. By Holy Cow Leather.

This waterformed leather shield utilizes several decorative techniques. The four rosettes were cut out of the surface and underlaid with suede. The detail (right) shows one of the four incised circles. The pattern was first traced with a dull point on slightly wet leather, then inked in—the outlines with drawing ink, and the colors with fine-tip, permanent ink markers. By John Solins, Amaranth Leather, Hatfield, Massachusetts.

8

Carving

Traditionally, the technique of leather carving has been combined with tooling to produce the detailed floral patterns of "Western" leather. In this chapter, however, we're going to show you how to create modern carved designs, using simple woodcarving tools.

Woodcarving tools are used to gouge or channel the surface of the leather in much the same way as with wood. V-shaped tools produce deep, narrow channels, and U-shaped tools, a wider, shallower channel.

Carving should be done after all pieces of a project are cut, holes punched, etc., but *before* the pieces are dyed, sewn, laced, or riveted. You might use an awl to lightly draw in your design before carving. (This isn't absolutely necessary, but will improve your control, especially when carving a complex design.) No special work area is needed for carving, but you may wish to cover the table with a thick layer of newspapers, scrap leather, wood, or some other protective material in case your hand slips.

MATERIALS

One V-shaped and one U-shaped tool are all that you will really need, but you might purchase a full set of woodcarving tools for a greater variety of effects. Use a thick leather, at least $5/6$ oz. in weight, with a smooth, hard surface. The thicker the leather, the deeper you'll be able to carve it, without cutting all the way through. Latigo can be carved, but shoulder and carving cowhide are even better.

PROBLEMS

If the leather tears through in later use, or while you're carving it, you're probably cutting too deeply with the tools. Lighten your pressure or use a heavier weight leather. Beware of soft spots in the leather which might tear or be cut through too easily.

If you find it difficult to get your tool to start cutting through the leather, or if your cuts are ragged rather than smooth, perhaps the blade of the tool has become dull. Sharpen it carefully with a fine file or replace the blade. Another possible cause of ragged edges on your cuts is soft leather. Try switching to a harder, stiffer leather and see if your lines improve.

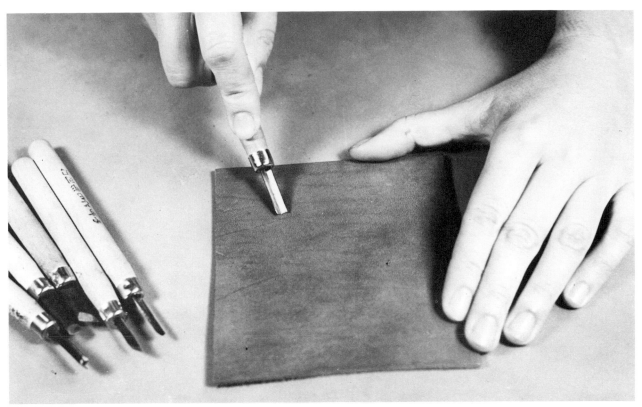

Step 1. *After you've planned your design and chosen the carving tools you'll need to execute it, try the tools out on scrap leather to see what they'll do. Hold the tool as shown here.*

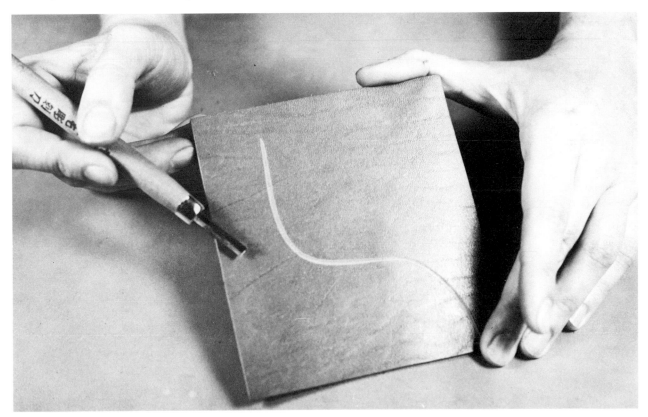

Step 2. *Place the tool on the leather, and push away from yourself, applying enough pressure to sink the sharp edge of the tool just under the surface of the leather. The desired result is a smooth, steady channel. Practice on leather scraps until you can control the depth and direction of the line; you should be able to draw lines, curves, etc., as needed to form your design.*

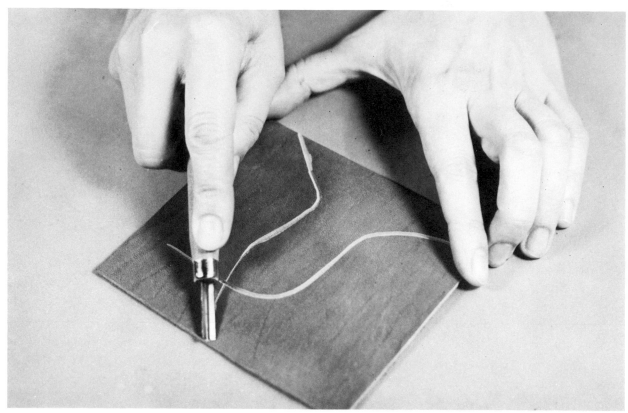

Step 3. *Change the pressure and twist the tool slightly from left to right for variations.*

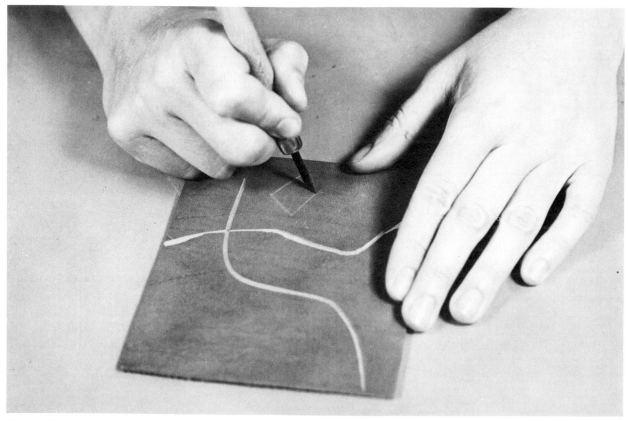

Step 4. *Whole flat areas may be carved out by first cutting the outline of the area with a flat-edged carving tool.*

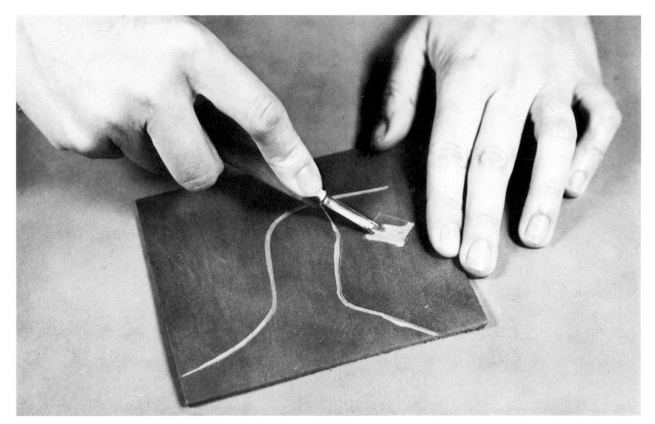

Step 5. *Use a wide-mouthed, U-shaped tool to scrape inwards from the outline, removing the top surface of the leather.*

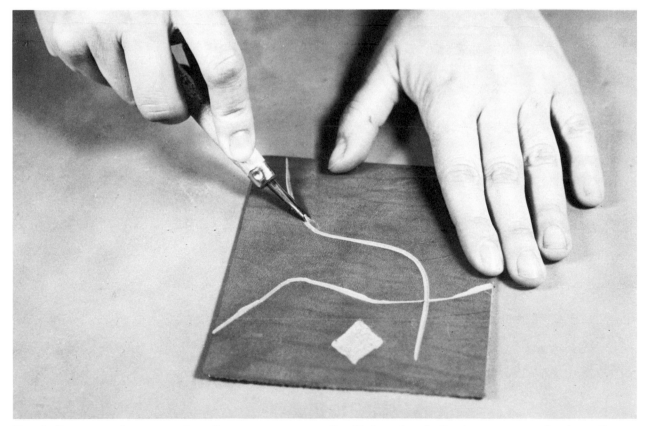

Step 6. *To cut out the center of smaller areas, use a smaller U-shaped tool. Don't gouge very deeply until you've removed the whole top surface. You can then go back over it, to make it deeper and to smooth out the rough spots.*

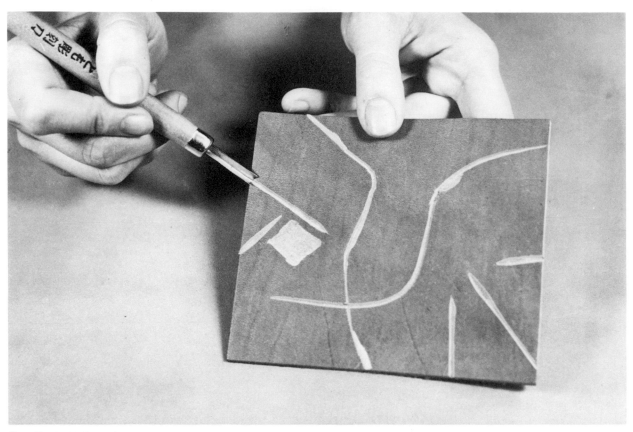

Step 7. *A V-shaped tool can be used to carve a fairly deep line.*

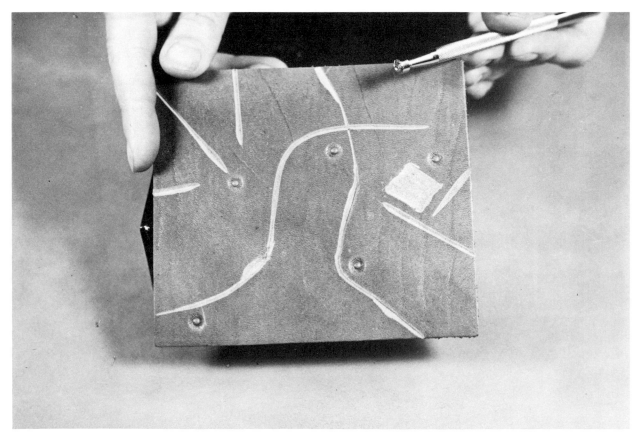

Step 8. *Combine stamping tools with your carved lines for interesting effects. For example, to make various flower and plant designs, you might carve the vines or stems, and stamp in the leaves or flowers.*

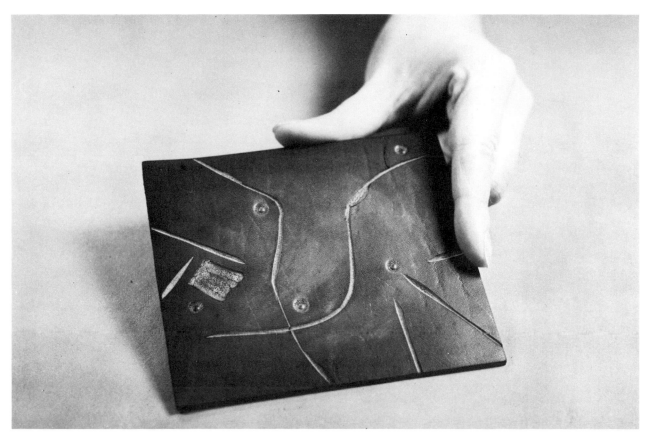

Step 9. *Use one or more of the dyeing methods demonstrated in Chapters 1–3 to enhance your carved design. You'll find more care is needed when dyeing over carved designs, in order to keep the dye from slipping into the recessed areas. Go gently and use a fairly dry rag. Even if you don't dye the piece, you should still saddle soap and possibly finish it, as described in Chapter 1.*

The tree design on this box was done with woodcarving tools, then the leather was shaded with dye. The box is made of leather and plywood. By David Warden, Ithaca, New York.

The design on this handbag was created by carving the spider web design, then highlighting the lines with dye. By Lee Harris, Belmont, Vermont.

9

Awl Drawing

The awl, known for such practical uses in leathercraft as marking and sketching designs, is today being recognized as a decorating tool also. Thanks to its fine point and ease of handling, the awl can be used to create many detailed, fine-lined designs. The awl is simply held in the hand and drawn across the leather like a pencil on paper, except that more pressure is required. It can be used by itself or combined with other processes such as stamping, tooling, and carving.

For example, to make a nature scene, use the awl to draw vines and stems, then stamp in flowers, leaves, and seeds. Or, combine awl lines with geometric stamping tools to create interesting abstract patterns.

Awl drawing should be done after all pieces of a project are cut, holes punched, etc., but *before* the pieces are dyed, painted, sewn, laced, or riveted. Place the piece of leather on a hard, smooth surface. If your worktable has holes or other depressions, and you place the leather directly over it, your awl will slip over these spots, causing an uneven line or possibly even a hole in the leather.

MATERIALS

We recommend that you use a stitching awl because it has a somewhat duller point than the standard workshop awl. A sharp-pointed awl *scratches* rather than *presses* lines into the leather. As for your leather, just about any with a smooth finish will do—kip, latigo, shoulder, tooling leather, etc.

PROBLEMS

If your awl line comes out ragged, you may be pressing too hard, or the leather you're using may be too soft. If your lines fade away, you're not pressing hard enough.

Step 1. *Hold the awl as you would a pencil.*

Step 2. *Press hard to cut a deep line across the leather; with practice, you'll be able to press very hard and still keep control over your lines. Awl drawing produces a subtle effect even when you press deeply, but a too-lightly drawn awl line will fade away, producing unsatisfactory results.*

Step 3. *For stippling effects, prick the leather many times with the point of the awl.*

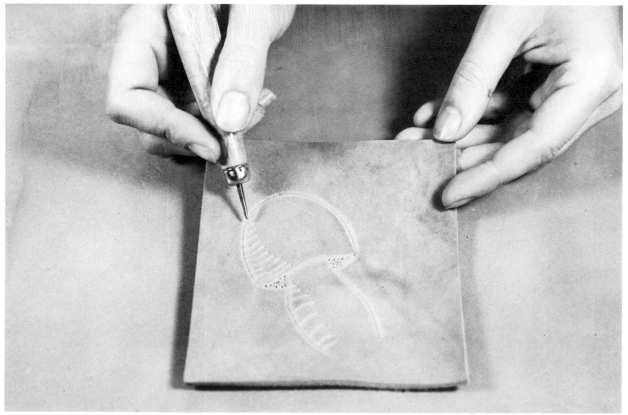

Step 4. *To create the effect of shading, draw parallel lines from the left edge of an object inward, about 1/4" or 1/3" across the surface, following the contour of the figure.*

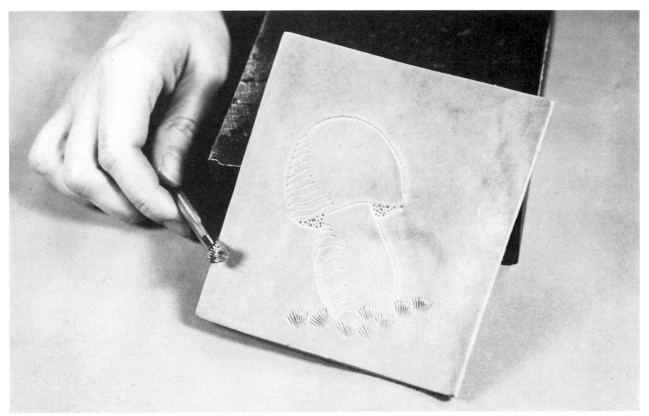

Step 5. *Awl drawing can be combined with stamping tools for some very interesting effects.*

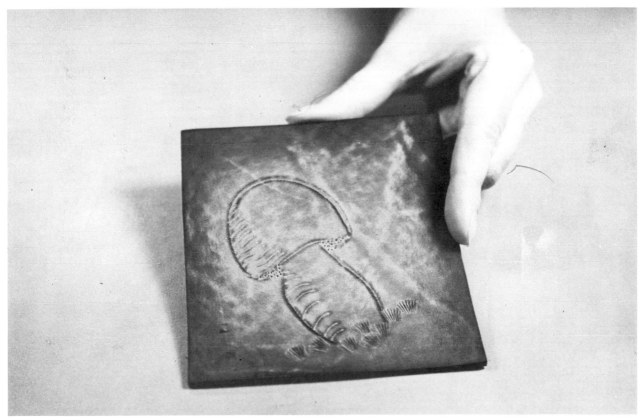

Step 6. *To further enrich your design, use one or more of the dyeing techniques discussed in Chapters 1–3. Great care should be taken, however, not to cover up the subtle awl lines. Experiment with various dyeing techniques until you find the one that best enhances the awl lines. Finally, saddle soap and finish the leather as described in Chapter 1, whether you have dyed it or not.*

The marks on the wings of this butterfly, made of 6/7 oz. shoulder, were drawn with an awl and dyed a different color than the rest of the wings. Pieces of dowel were used for antennae. By David Warden, Ithaca, New York.

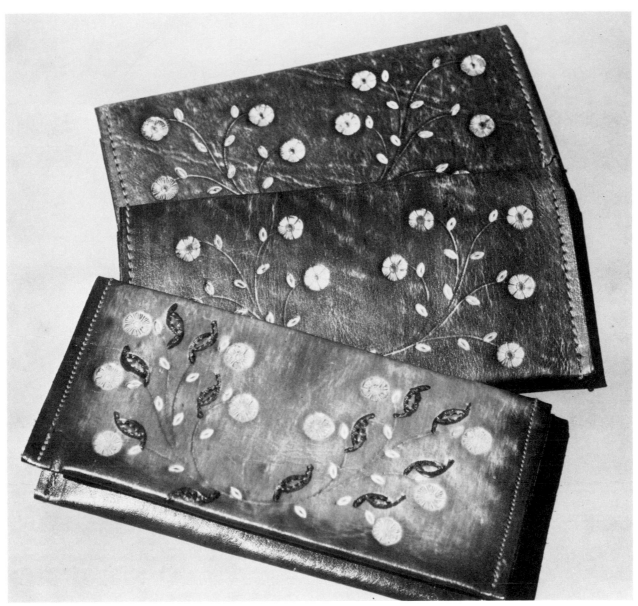

Each of these three wallets is made of 2/3 oz. English kip. The vines were drawn with an awl, while the flowers, leaves, and seeds were stamped in, then painted with brush and dye. The wallets were dyed overall in various solid colors. By Holy Cow Leather.

10

Leather Burning

Although burning is a technique traditionally used on wood, leather has proven to be as effective a medium. The tip of the burning tool is held against the leather until it begins to burn the surface, leaving a dark brown mark. Drawing the tip slowly across the leather leaves a line; varying the tip, pressure applied, and amount of time the tip is held in one place changes the character of the lines—thin or thick, shallow or deep. The end results of leather burning are more subtle than stamping or carving, because the burn lines blend naturally into the brown leather tones.

Leather burning should be done after all pieces of a project are cut, holes punched, etc., but *before* the pieces are sewn, laced, or riveted.

MATERIALS

1. A wood burner with 2 or more tips of different widths and shapes.
2. An electrical outlet.

Choose a good quality wood (or leather) burner, one that is UL approved for electrical safety. Some burners come with a stand to rest the burner on when not in use—this is good to have. Latigo, kip, tooling, and carving leather are fine, although suede and highly finished leathers won't work well. Use a light-colored leather or your burn lines won't show up.

PROBLEMS

If you find it difficult to draw an even, deep line across the leather, it may be that your burner has not warmed up enough. Or, the leather you're using may have a highly glazed finish. Try the burner on another kind of leather.

If your burner puts holes right through the leather, you may be pressing too hard or leaving the tip in one spot too long. Another possibility is that you're using leather which is too thin.

Step 1. *Hold the burner in your hand just like a pencil. Be careful not to hold it too close to the hot tip.*

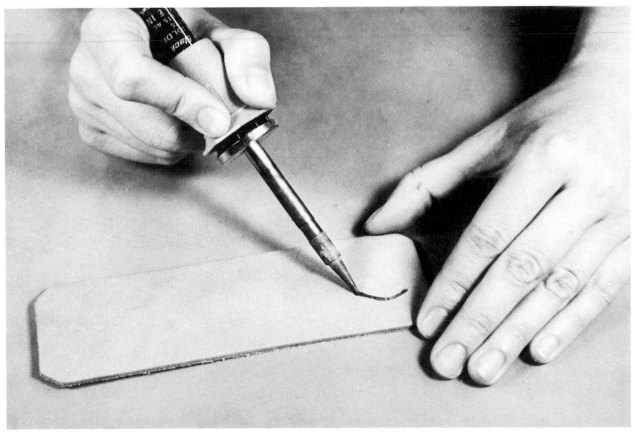

Step 2. *Draw with the burner as you would with a pen, but moving it much more slowly, giving the tip a chance to burn into the leather.*

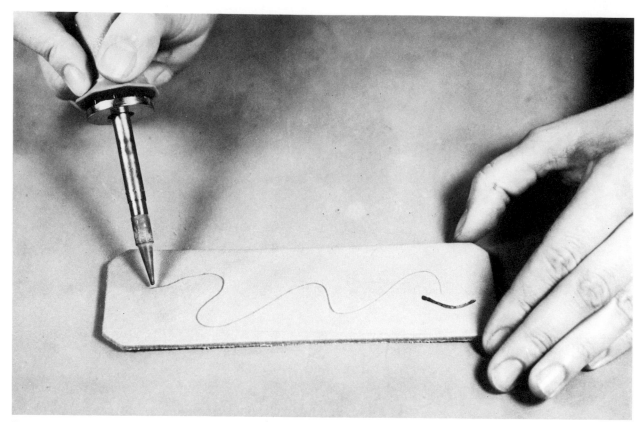

Step 3. *A quick stroke across the leather will leave a light, shallow line.*

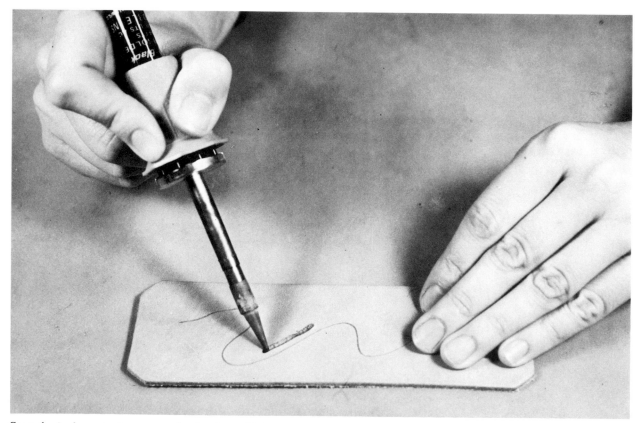

Step 4. *A slow stroke across the leather will leave a darker, deeper line.*

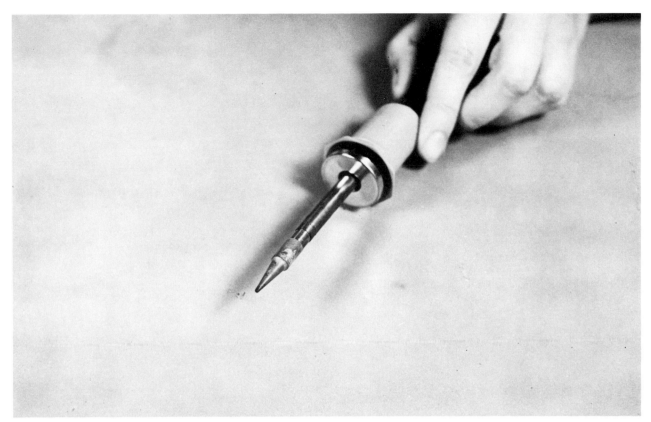

Step 5. *A standard pointed tip is best for line drawing, because all the heat is concentrated in the point, providing the most efficient drawing tool.*

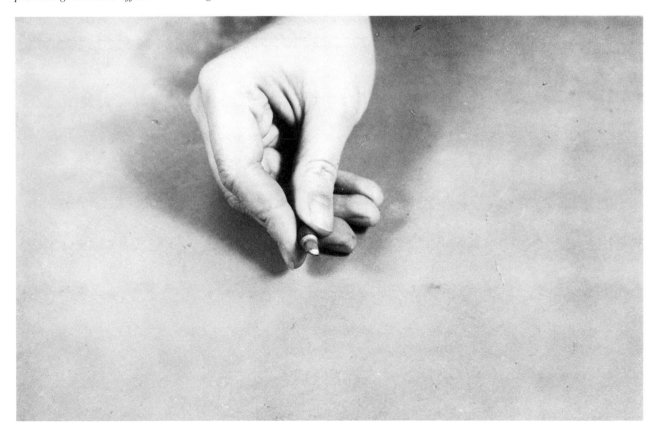

Step 6. *Some tips have wide, flat surfaces which can be used for other effects. These will have to be held on the leather for a longer period of time, and with more pressure, than the pointed tip. Experiment with various tips on scrap leather to discover what each one can do.*

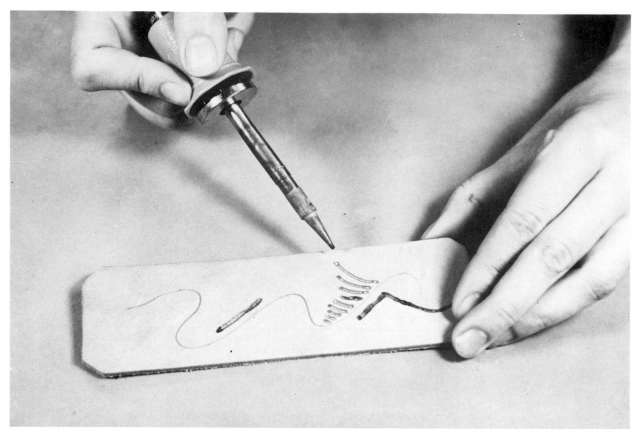

Step 7. *To create the effect of shading with the pointed tip, draw parallel lines from the left edge of an outline inward, about ¼ to ⅓ of the way across its surface, following the contour of the figure.*

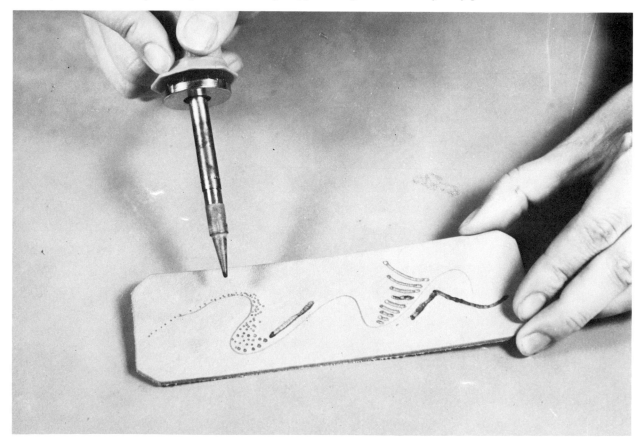

Step 8. *For stippled effects, touch the pointed tip of the burner repeatedly to the surface of the leather.*

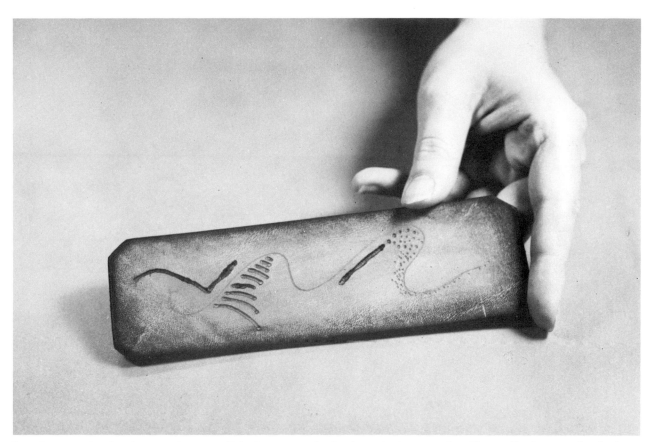

Step 9. *Since leather burning leaves a light image on the leather, dyeing over it will usually destroy the design. Therefore, we suggest only a light shading around the edge of the piece of leather. Don't use dye directly on the burned areas. Another approach is to use a very light-colored dye such as yellow, but this may still dull the burn lines. Or, you may wish to dye the leather* first *and* then *burn in your design. This will produce a more subtle effect than burning an undyed, light-colored leather. Of course, you might simply saddle soap and finish the piece as described in Chapter 1, without dyeing it at all.*

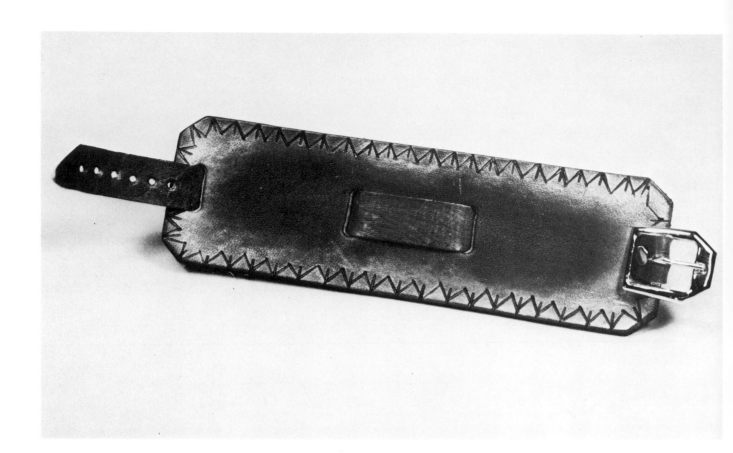

This watchband (above) was made of 6/7 oz. russet shoulder. The design along the edge of the band was marked with a wood burner, then the center of the band was dyed brown. By Lyn Taetzsch.

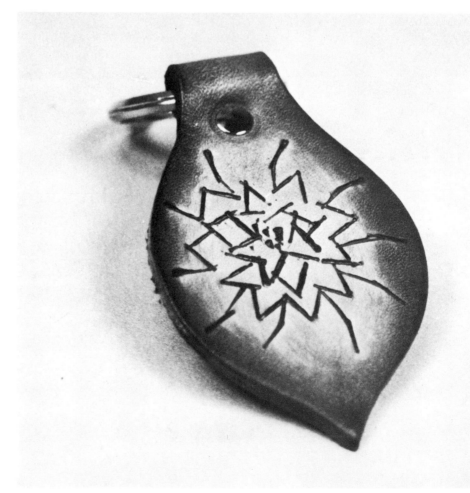

First, the design on this keyring was done with a wood burner; then the edges of the ring were lightly shaded. By Lyn Taetzsch.

*The design on this 1 3/4"
belt (above) was made with
a wood burner, and the
edges of the leather were
lightly shaded. By Lyn
Taetzsch.*

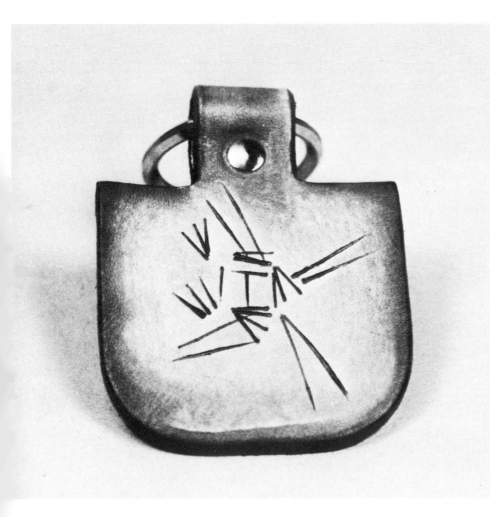

*A wood burner was used to
make the design on this
keyring, and the edges of the
ring were lightly shaded
with dye. By Lyn Taetzsch.*

11

Appliqué

The technique of appliqué can be used on all kinds of leather to decorate just about any item you make, from bookmarks to handbags to furniture. An appliqué is a cutout decoration fastened to a larger piece of material by a variety of means—gluing, stitching, or riveting. Two or more appliqués may be fastened to the same piece of leather, in different areas, or one on top of the other. Appliqué offers limitless decorative possibilities, and can be combined with other techniques, such as dyeing and shading. However, appliqué should be done after all pieces of a project are cut, holes punched, etc., and before the pieces are sewn, laced, or riveted.

MATERIALS

1. Leather glue.
2. A brush for stroking on glue.
3. Rivets.
4. A rivet setter.
5. Rawhide mallet.
6. A hole punch for riveting.
7. Sewing machine, or, if you prefer, a stitching awl.
8. Utility knife and/or scissors.
9. Drawing awl.

You'll need enough leather for your basic project plus the appliqués, or you can use one type of leather for the project and another for the appliqués. Any kind of leather can be used for appliqué —garment, cowhide, suede, glove.

Most standard sewing machines can be used to sew thin leather, such as suede. Follow your machine instructions manual for tension settings, type of needle to use, etc. Practice on scrap pieces of leather first. Before you begin to sew your appliqué, glue it to the object, then stitch carefully around the outer edge, about ⅛″ from the perimeter of the cutout.

If you plan to stitch the appliqué by hand, purchase a leather stitching awl and follow the directions that come with it. You may have to punch holes before stitching, except with very thin leather. So, glue the pieces together first, mark the holes with an awl, punch them with a #0 hole punch, and stitch.

To rivet an appliqué to your project piece, follow the basic riveting procedure outlined later, in Chapter 14.

PROBLEMS

If a glued appliqué design starts to peel off after a while, you may need to use a better quality glue, or add rivets and/or stitching for additional strength.

If your appliqué is attached with one rivet in the center, and it begins to turn rather than staying firm, hit the rivet setter over the rivet again to tighten it up.

If your rivets come apart, you may have hit them crooked or not hard enough. If they're crooked, take the parts out and start again with new rivets.

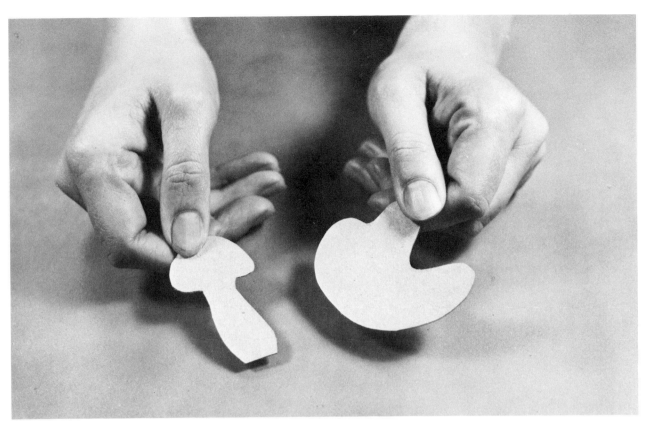

Step 1. *First, plan your appliqué design and make a paper pattern for each of the cutouts. If you plan more than one layer of appliqué, each additional layer should be smaller than the piece under it. This will give a three-dimensional layered effect which is quite striking. Place the paper patterns on your project to check your design before cutting it out of leather.*

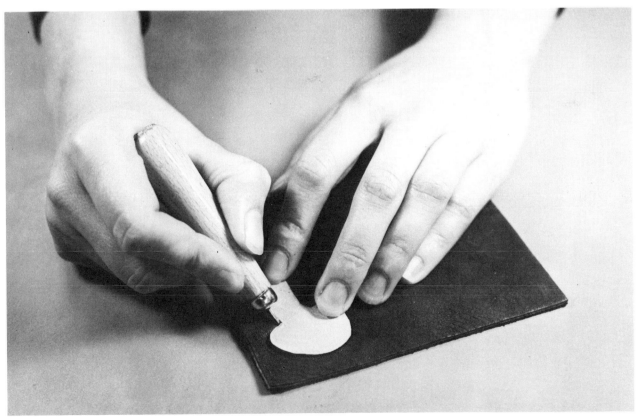

Step 2. *Next, trace each pattern on the appliqué leather with an awl.*

Step 3. *Carefully cut out the pieces, using a scissors for thin leather such as suede or kip, and a utility knife for heavy leather such as cowhide.*

Step 4. *When cutting straight edges, a ruler can be used as a guide to keep your knife on the awl line.*

Step 5. *Place the leather cutouts on the project piece to see how they will look. You may want to lightly trace their outline with an awl, so you can later replace them in their proper positions.*

Step 6. *Use a brush to lightly coat the back of the appliqués.*

Step 7. *Stroke a light coat of glue on the project piece also, being careful to apply it only to the area that will be covered by the cutout.*

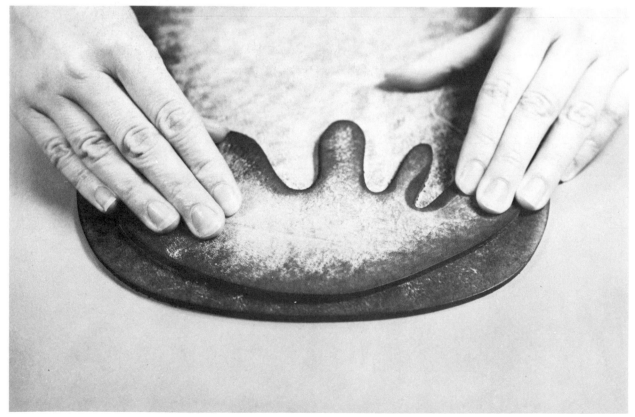

Step 8. *Let the glue dry until it's tacky, then carefully place the cutout on the project piece and press firmly. Allow to dry thoroughly.*

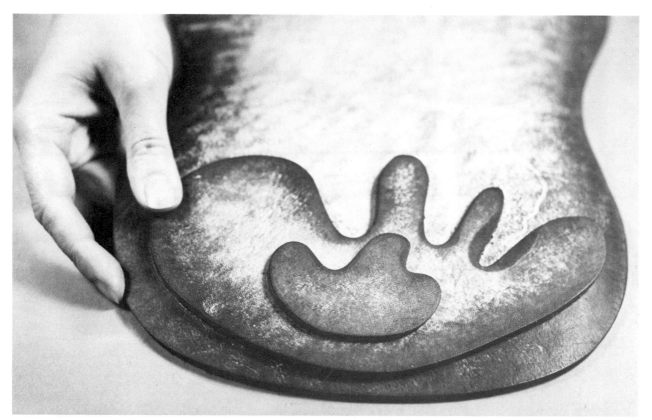

Step 9. *Two or more layers of appliqué give an interesting three-dimensional effect to your project.*

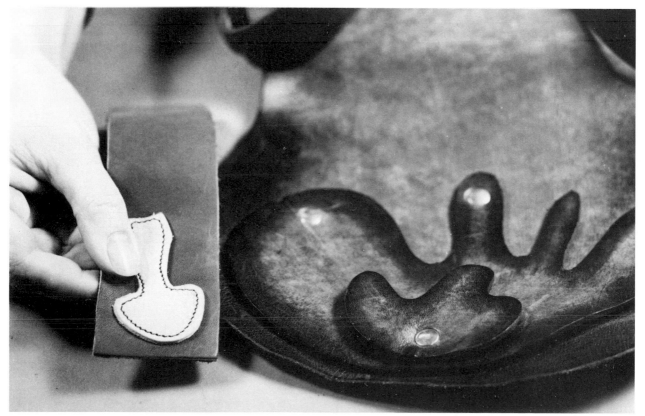

Step 10. *We suggest stitching or riveting your appliqué to the project piece—while giving your project a decorative touch, these techniques also provide additional strength. Stitching is best used on thin leather and riveting on heavier leather.*

The mushroom appliqué on this handbag was cut from the reverse side of the calico-flesh cowhide used for the rest of this bag. The edges of the appliqué were dyed before it was glued and sewn to the front flap of the bag. By Holy Cow Leather.

The appliqué on this handbag of machine-stitched, calico-flesh cowhide is the reverse side of the leather used for the rest of bag. This provides an interesting contrast in textures. By Holy Cow Leather.

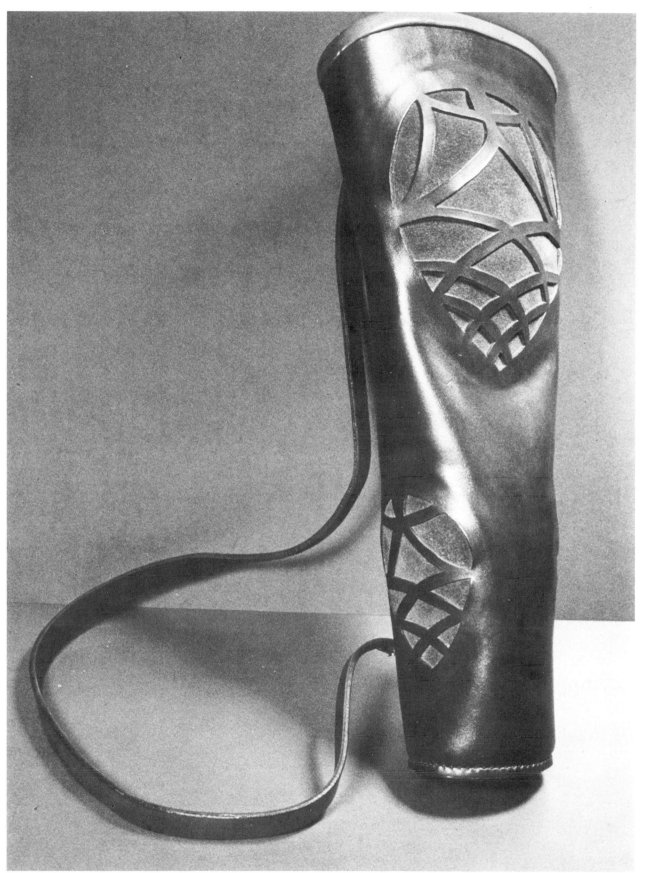

The decorative effects on this quiver were made by cutting out sections of the body (4 oz. vegetable tanned leather), and underlying them with suede. The seams were hand stitched. By Jon Solins, Amaranth Leather, Hatfield, Massachusetts.

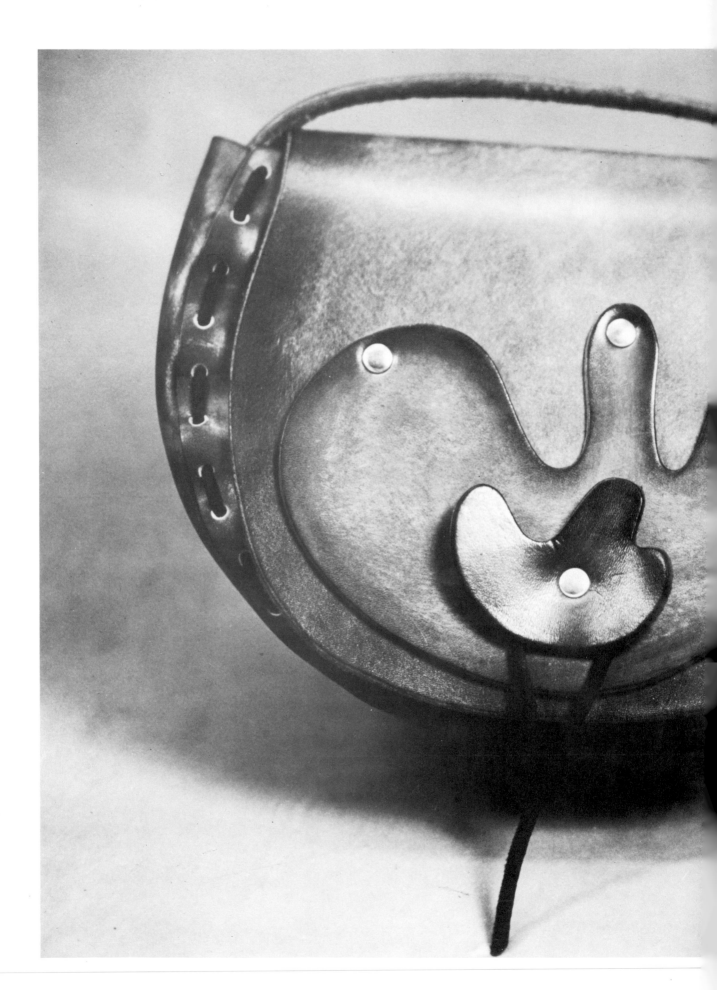

This handbag is made of 6/7 oz. russet shoulder and hand laced with 1/8'' black latigo lacing. The front flap is decorated with an abstract appliqué made of two pieces of leather riveted to it. All parts of the bag were dyed red and shaded with burgundy. The smaller appliqué piece also provides a catch for closing. By Holy Cow Leather.

12

Decorative Hole Punching

Decorative hole punching has been very popular on leather belts, but can be used effectively on almost any leather project such as watchbands, wristbands, barrettes, handbags, clothing, and so forth. It's important to limit the number and size of the holes in order to maintain the strength of the leather, but once this precaution has been met, many interesting results can be achieved.

The technique consists simply of holding a hole punch on the leather and hitting the punch squarely with a mallet to make a hole through the leather. Hole punches are available in various sizes and shapes. Larger holes can be cut with a utility knife. The arrangement of the holes forms a pattern which "decorates" the leather project. The holes can be left open for air, skin, or whatever is behind them to show through, or another material may be glued to the back to show through the holes.

Leather of a contrasting texture or color, burlap, canvas, metal, and wood, are just some of the many materials that make interesting backing material. Naturally, if the leather project is to be worn, or for some other reason must be flexible, you'll have to use a flexible backing material. Or, you might instead use small pieces of wood or other hard materials to cover only one hole at a time. Of course, some holes can be covered while others are left open, and so forth. Backing material may also be required for additional strength. If the project is made from a thin leather, with many holes, the backing material will make it stronger and keep the holes from stretching.

Decorative hole punching should be done after all pieces of a project are cut, dyed, saddle soaped, and finished, but before they are sewn, laced, or riveted. If you try to dye the pieces *after* punching the holes, it will be difficult to dye around the holes.

MATERIALS

1. Hole punches of various sizes and/or shapes.
2. Rawhide mallet.
3. Drawing awl.
4. Ruler.
5. Some heavy scrap leather or rubber.
6. A chopping block or a 2″ thick steel plate.
7. Utility knife.
8. Your choice of backing materials.
9. Glue.

Decorative hole punching can be done on any kind of leather from thin suede to heavy cowhide.

PROBLEMS

If the holes in your final project stretch or tear with use, it could be you're using too thin a leather or making too many and too large holes. One remedy is to apply a backing material for additional strength.

If your holes don't come out clean, your hole punches may be dull. Use a file to sharpen them, or buy new ones. When cutting with a utility knife, start with a new blade for best results.

Step 1. *First plan your hole pattern and try the design on a piece of scrap leather. Then, using a ruler and an awl, measure the distance between holes and mark them off on your project piece of leather.*

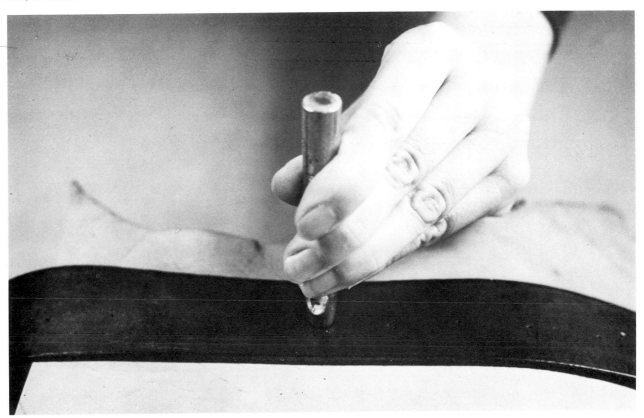

Step 2. *If you're using round hole punches, place the heavy scrap leather or rubber over the steel plate, with the piece you want to punch on top. This way, when your punch cuts through the top piece of leather, it will hit the rubber or scrap leather rather than the steel plate—which would dull the tool faster. Hold the punch firmly in your left hand (vice versa if you're left-handed).*

Step 3. *Hit the punch squarely with the rawhide mallet. It may take more than one hit to cut through, depending on the thickness of the leather, the strength of your blow, the size of the hole desired, and the sharpness of the hole punch.*

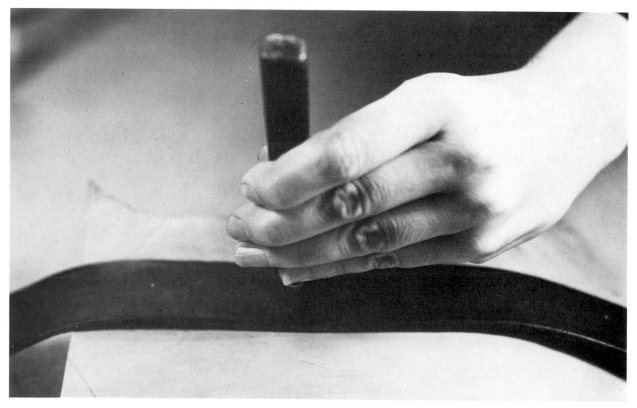

Step 4. *If you're using an oblong bag punch (especially a large one, such as 1 or 1-1/2"), more effort may be required to cut through the leather. After you make your first hit, rock the tool slightly forward and hit it with the mallet. Then rock the tool slightly backward and hit again. Be sure to hold the punch in the same spot at all times, however, or your hole won't be clean.*

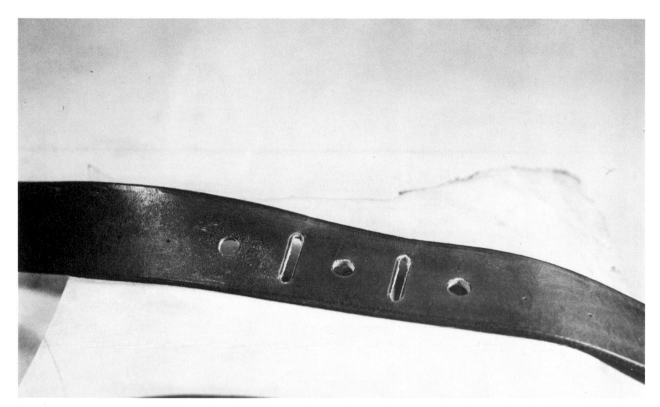

Step 5. *Decorative hole punching should be done after the leather has been dyed; round and oblong holes alternate in this belt.*

Step 6. *Hole punching can be enhanced by gluing a backing material to the leather so it will show through the holes. (Use the same procedure as that for gluing an appliqué to leather, described in Chapter 10.) Of course, hole punching can also be combined with appliqué and complemented by backing materials for very striking three-dimensional effects.*

Step 1. *Odd-sized holes, for which you can't buy a punch, can be outlined with an awl, then cut out. Large circles should be first drawn with a compass, before you outline them with an awl.*

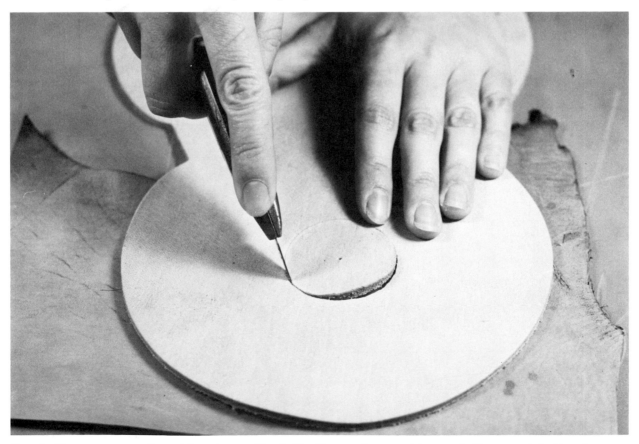

Step 2. *Cut out your outline with a sharp utility knife. Use a ruler to guide your knife on straight-line shapes.*

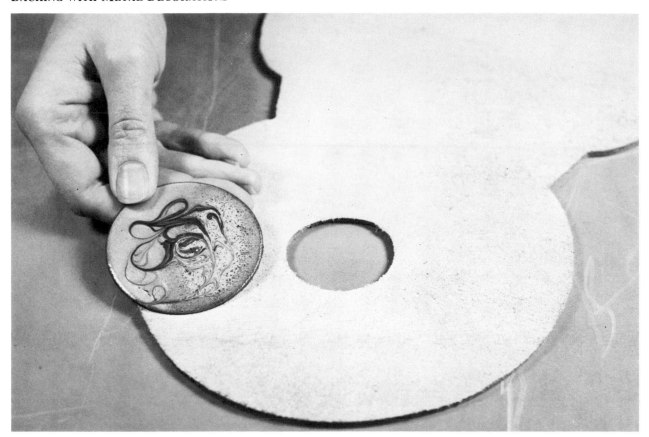

Step 1. To attach a piece of metal or other material which may not hold with glue alone, lay your project piece face down on the table.

Step 2. Place the backing metal or other object over the hole so that it overlaps about 1/8 –1/4".

Step 3. *Cut a piece of thin leather 1/2–1" larger than the metal.*

Step 4. *Glue the thin piece of leather over the metal to the back of the project, using the appliqué gluing method described in Chapter 10.*

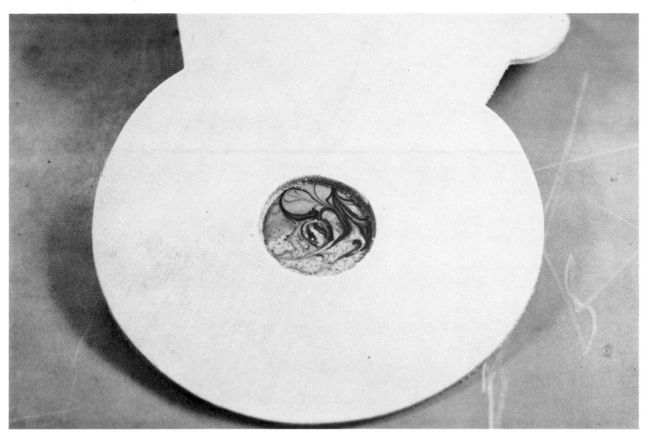

Step 5. *The metal design shows through the hole in the project piece.*

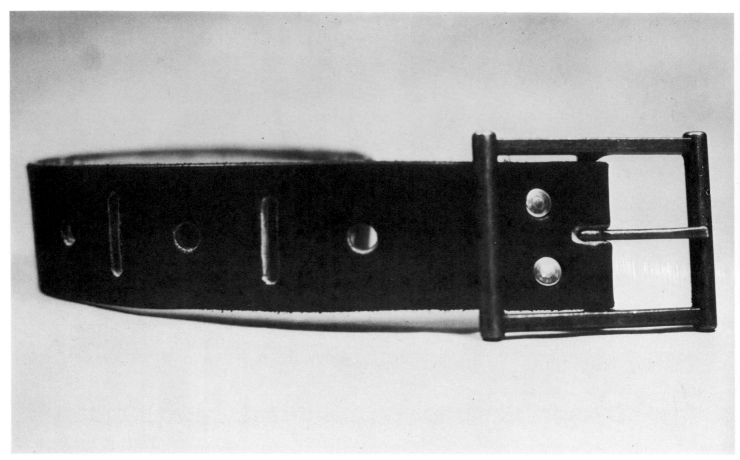

After this belt was dyed an overall shade of brown, the interesting round and oblong hole design was punched. By Holy Cow Leather.

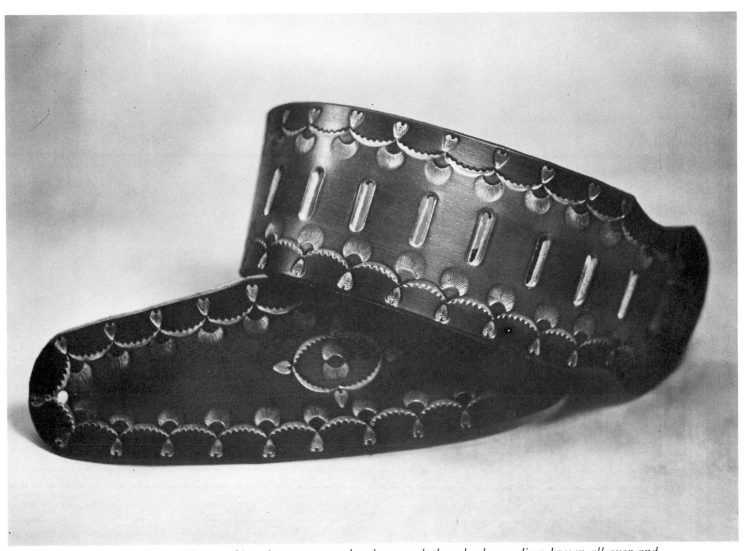

Made of 6/7 oz. neutral latigo, this guitar strap was hand stamped, then dyed a medium brown all over and shaded with dark brown on the edges. The strap has been given a thorough saddle soaping and two coats of harness dressing to produce a polished finish. By John Cowan.

13

Stitching and Lacing

Although stitching and lacing are a practical means of assembling your project, they also add to the decorative effect of the piece. Therefore it's important to consider not only which method is the strongest and most efficient, but also which assembly method will *look* best. In fact, stitching and lacing may be used for purely decorative effects even when not needed for practical purposes.

Check your machine manual for instructions on sewing leather. Usually the tension will have to be adjusted, a longer stitch used, and a special leather needle necessary. Begin with thin garment leathers or single layers of leather to see if your machine can handle it. If your stitching will be used to hold an article together, such as a wallet or purse, use a strong thread or the article will tear apart later. If your machine does zigzag and other decorative stitching, use colored thread and experiment with designs to decorate vests, bookmarks, pouches, and other items made of soft, thin leather. For heavier leathers, you'll need a heavy-duty or industrial machine.

To do hand lacing, you punch holes through the leather, then draw the lace in and out through the holes, pulling it tight along the way, and knotting at the end. There are many lacing techniques which are explained in detail in some of the leathercraft books on the market. We're going to cover two simple methods in this book—straight and crisscross lacing. Both these methods can be used with heavy leather, such as latigo, or with a thinner leather, such as suede. After you have mastered them, you can then experiment to discover new techniques or read other books for more ideas.

MATERIALS

1. Round hole punches, #0–4.
2. Rawhide mallet.
3. Lace.
4. A lacing needle.

If you're lacing heavy leather such as $^6/_7$ oz. or $^7/_8$ oz. latigo or shoulder, use ⅛″ rawhide or latigo laces. These can be purchased in various colors, or you can dye them yourself by sticking the laces a few at a time in a bottle of dye, pulling them out slowly, and letting them dry on newspaper. Dye all pieces before lacing, being careful to dye the edges of the pieces which will show after lacing. For moccasins, a heavy wax thread will work best. For suede and other soft leathers, buy or make lace out of similar material. There are various lacing needles available for these thinner, softer laces, and, of course, depending on the width of the lace, you may need to punch smaller or larger holes.

PROBLEMS

If, when the bag is finished, the lacing looks loose and the bag pieces separate, you must pull more tightly after each hole when lacing. Loose lacing is one of the most common beginner lacing errors. On the other hand, some people overdo it, and the bag ends up all puckered because it's too tight.

If the lace won't pull through the holes easily, try saddle soaping the lace first to make it smoother. Or, punch slightly larger holes.

Step 1. First, mark off matching holes on the gusset (or sides), and the front and back pieces. The holes should be anywhere from 1/2–3/4" apart and there must be an even number of holes on each piece for the lacing to come out right.

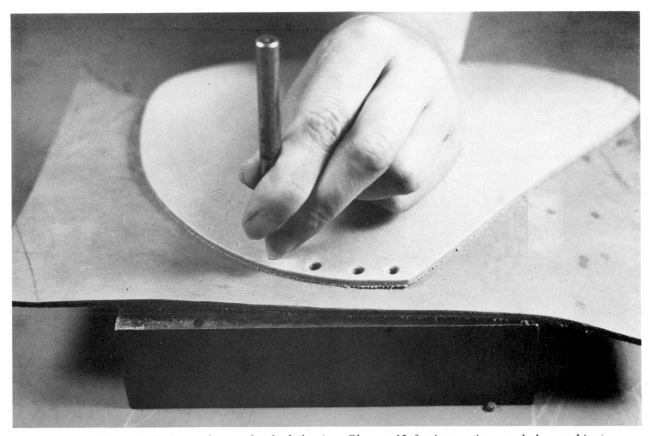

Step 2. Use a #3 or #4 hole punch to make the holes (see Chapter 12 for instructions on hole punching).

Step 3. *To thread a latigo life-eye needle, first cut the end of the lace at a diagonal to form a point.*

Step 4. *Screw the needle onto the latigo point by turning it in a clockwise direction. When the needle is screwed on tightly, you're ready to lace.*

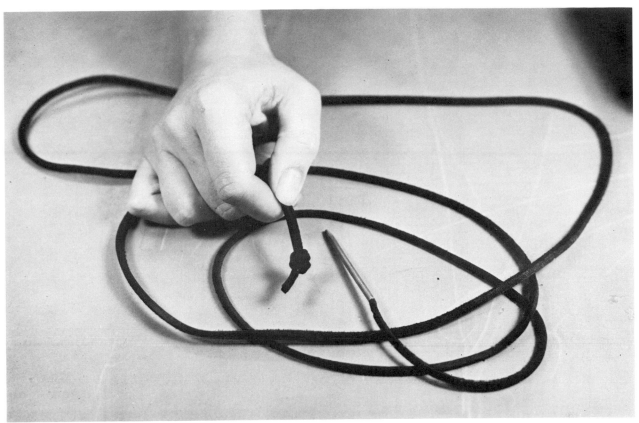

Step 5. *Tie a simple knot in the end of the lace and pull it tight.*

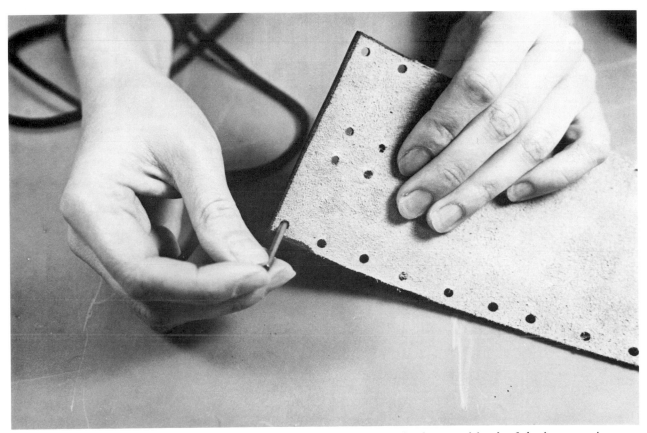

Step 6. *Decide ahead of time whether you want the gusset to overlap the front and back of the bag, or vice versa. In this case, we'll have the bag front and back overlap the gusset. Begin by drawing the lace through the back of the first gusset hole.*

Step 7. *Now push the needle up through the back of the first hole in the bag front, and draw the lace through.*

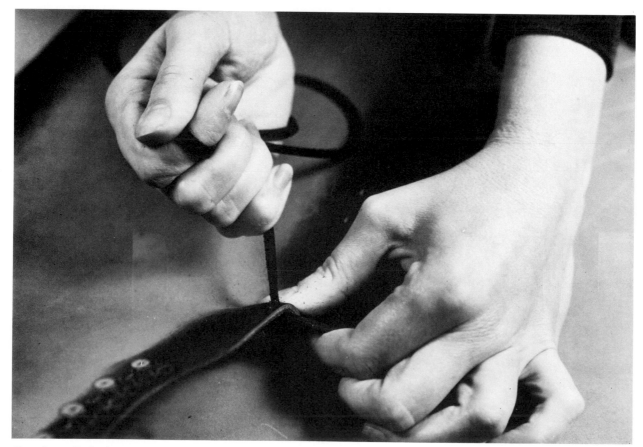

Step 8. *Pull the lace as tightly as you can against the back of the gusset.*

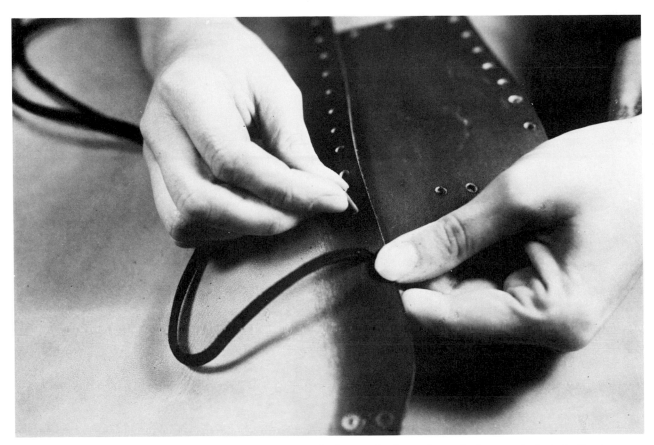

Step 9. *Holding the bag front and gusset together, push the needle down through the next hole in both pieces.*

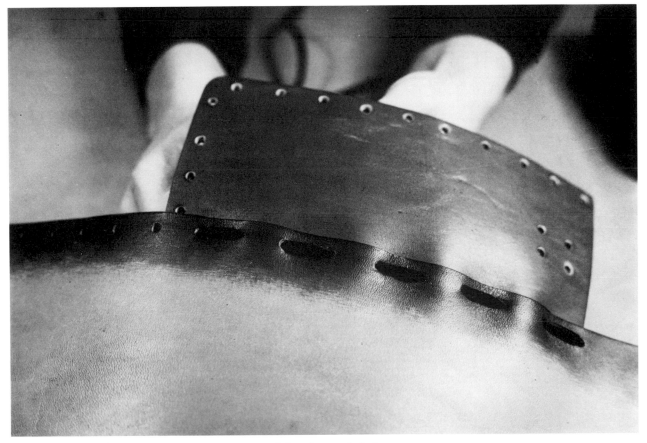

Step 10. *Continue lacing in and out, pulling tightly after each hole.*

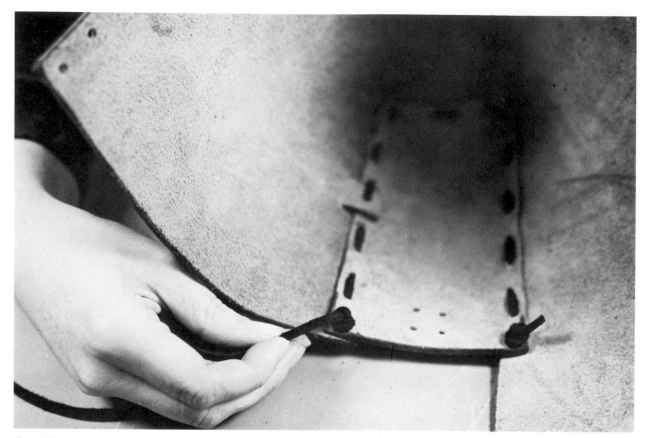

Step 11. *When you reach the end (you should end up on the inside of the bag), pull very tightly, then tie a knot up close to the leather.*

Step 1. *For crisscross lacing, punch the holes in the gusset, and front and back of the bag, as described above. Then butt the ends of the gusset and bag pieces together rather than overlapping them.*

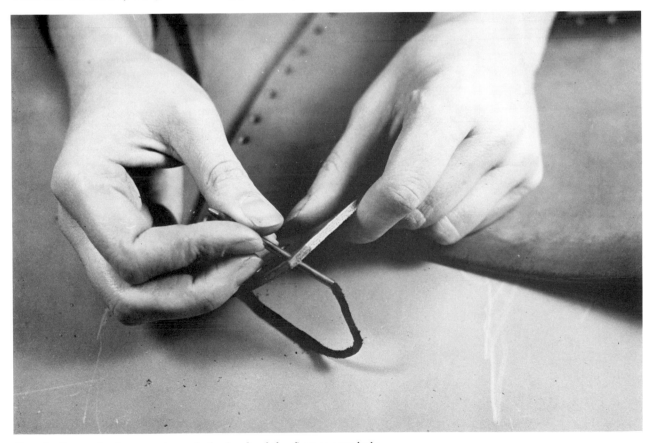

Step 2. *Draw the lace up through the back of the first gusset hole.*

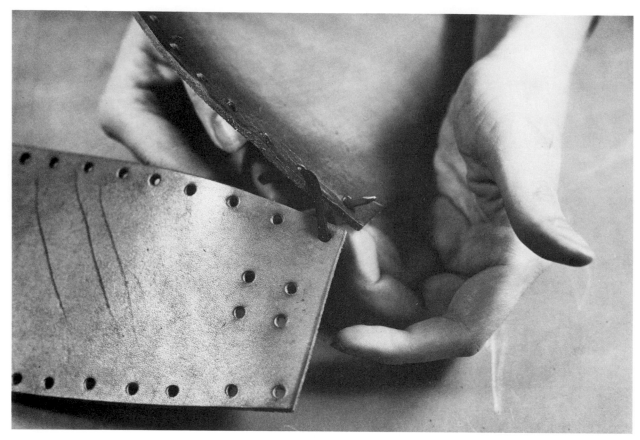

Step 3. *Then cross over and push the lace down through the second hole in the bag front.*

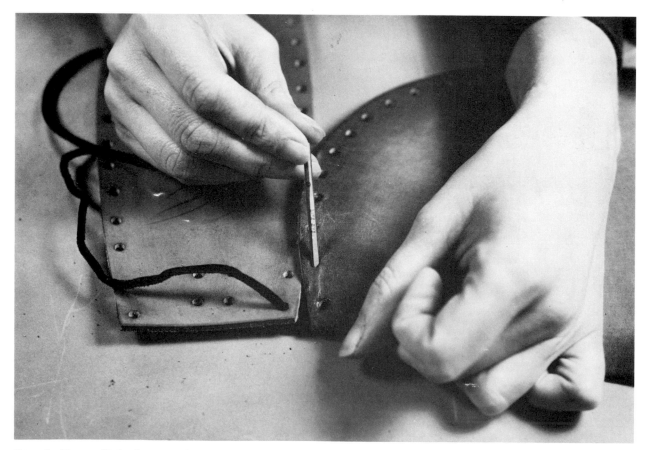

Step 4. *Now pull the lace up through the first hole in the bag front.*

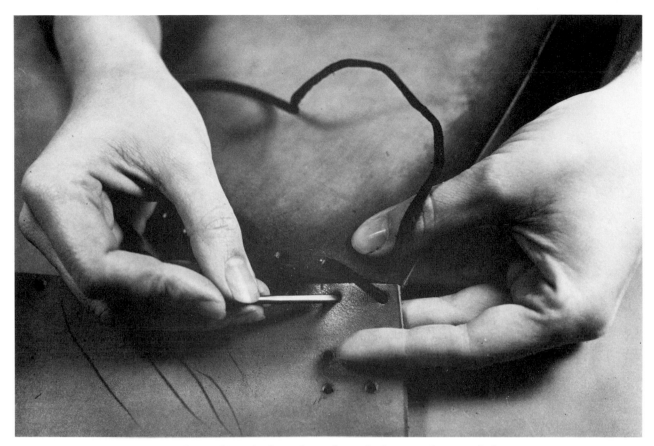

Step 5. *Finish your crisscross by pushing the lace down through the second gusset hole.*

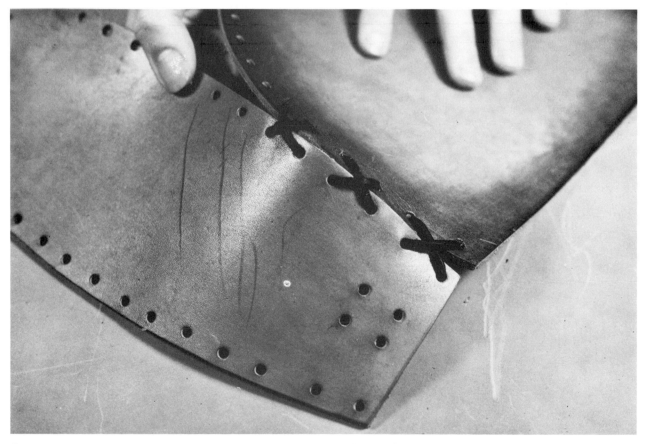

Step 6. *If you continue to lace as shown here, you should end up with a series of X's all around the bag.*

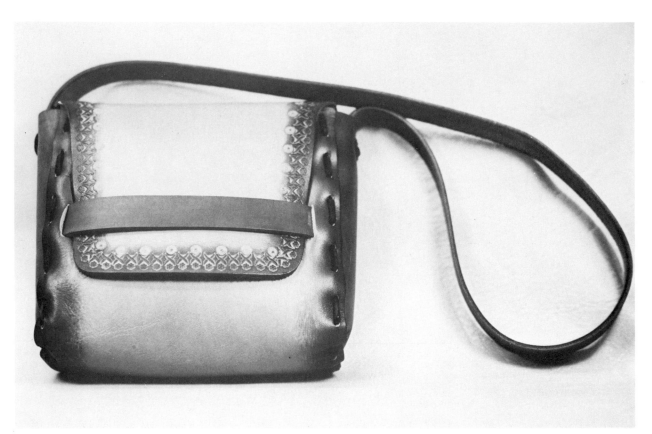

The design on the edge of the front flap of this bag was stamped in, then lightly shaded with dye. The bag, made of 6/7 oz. russet shoulder, has a front strap and latigo lacing.

The design on the front flap of this latigo handbag was stamped into the leather, then the outer edge of the flap was dyed darker than the rest of the bag. This bag also has a front strap and latigo lacing.

This handbag is basically made of deer-tanned cowhide. The top piece of latigo was stamped, painted, and shaded with dye, then glued and stitched to the soft leather. Notice the crisscross lacing along the gusset. By Holy Cow Leather.

Note the decorative effect of the turnlock closing on this handbag, and the use of rings to attach the shoulder strap. The handbag was machine stitched from soft, 4-5 oz. calico-flesh cowhide.

This handbag was machine stitched from soft, 4-5 oz. calico flesh cowhide. Note the decorative closing.

14

Rivets, Spots, Studs, and Rhinestones

Traditionally, rivets were used for practical purposes such as attaching a buckle to a belt, a strap to a handbag, etc. But rivets, which are available in nickel, gilt, antique brass, and brass, and in many sizes with round or flat heads, also have a decorative function. Add to rivets spots, studs, and rhinestones in their various styles and colors, and you've got an unlimited array of decorative possibilities.

Most rivets come in two parts—male and female. The male part is pushed up through a small hole in the leather and the female part placed over it. A rivet setter is pounded against the rivet so the male part spreads out inside the female part, forming a tight grip on the leather. Knobby rivets are also available, but cannot be set in the same manner as flat rivets. Tandy Leather Company (see Suppliers List) sells some which are simply squeezed between the forefinger and thumb to fasten. There are hand-operated machines that set rivets and spots; these can be purchased for $20 to $50.

Spots, studs, and rhinestones have two long prongs, which are pushed through leather and folded flat on the other side. Spots can be pushed through and flattened against thin leather rather easily by hand. On heavy leather, you'll have to start the holes by cutting a small slit with a utility knife or pushing a hole through with an awl. A small machine or handsetter is useful for attaching studs and rhinestones, although different settings must be used for each. (Follow the directions that come with the machine.)

Decorative riveting should be done after all pieces of a project are cut, carved, tooled, dyed, etc., but before they're assembled.

MATERIALS

1. #1 hole punch.
2. Rawhide mallet.
3. Drawing awl.
4. Utility knife.
5. A chopping block or a 2″ thick steel plate.
6. Some heavy scrap leather or rubber.
7. Rivet setter.
8. An assortment of rivets, spots, studs, and rhinestones.
9. Rhinestone handsetter or machine.

Rhinestones and studs will only work on thin leather such as suede, glove, garment leather, and kip. For heavier leathers, use rivets and spots.

PROBLEMS

If your rivets come apart or are loose, you may not be hitting the rivet setter hard enough. Or you may have left the scrap leather or rubber under the piece by mistake. The rivet must be set on a hard surface to work properly.

If the head of your rivet gets a crimp in it, you're not holding the setter directly centered over the top. Reposition the rivet setter.

If your studs and rhinestones fall out after you've attached them, you may be using a leather that's too thick. Their short prongs need enough room to bend over flat, in order to hold the stud or rhinestone in place.

Step 1. *Mark your rivet design with an awl. Use a ruler to measure the distance between rivets.*

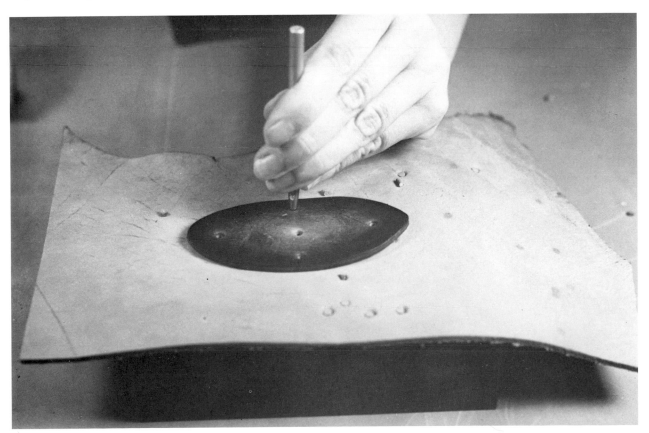

Step 2. *Punch a #1 hole for each rivet. (See Chapter 12 for instructions on hole punching.) When all the holes have been punched, remove the rubber or scrap leather from under the project piece, but keep the piece on the steel plate.*

Step 3. *Push the male rivet part up through a hole.*

Step 4. *Fit the female rivet part over the male part.*

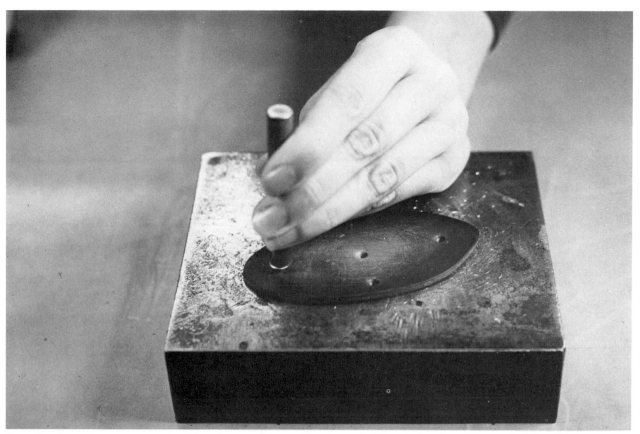

Step 5. *Place the concave end of the rivet setter over the rivet, holding it firmly with your left hand (vice versa if you're left-handed).*

Step 6. *Hit the setter squarely on the head with the mallet.*

Step 7. *Continue with each rivet until your design is complete.*

Step 1. *To put spots on thin leather, push the long prongs through the leather.*

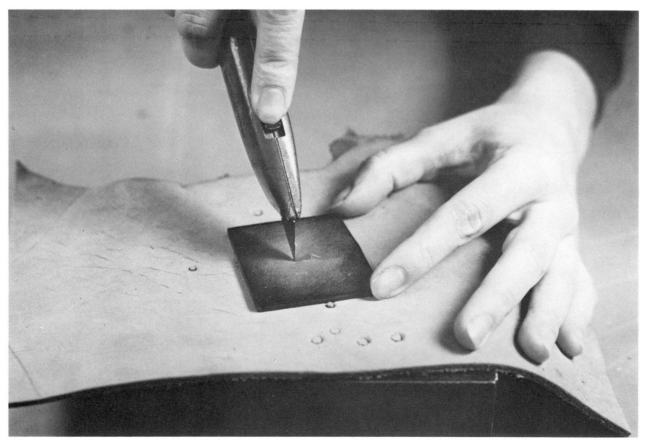

Step 2. *On heavy leather, cut two small slits in the leather the distance apart of the spot prongs.*

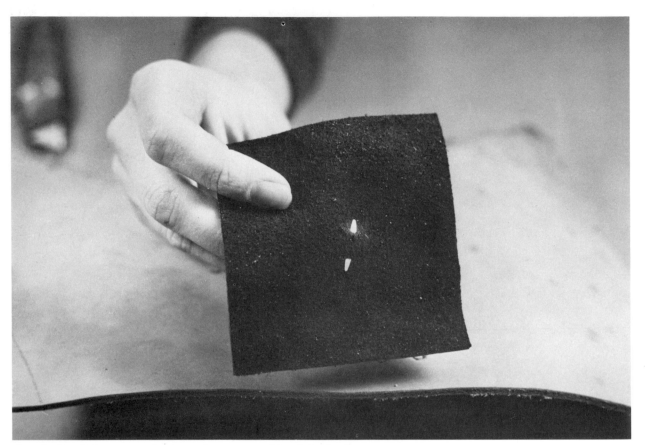

Step 3. *Bend the prongs back on the reverse side of the leather.*

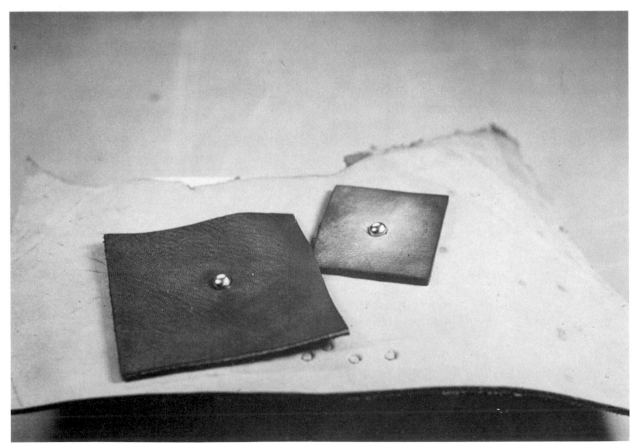

Step 4. *Now the spots are firmly attached.*

Step 1. *To decorate with rhinestones, mark your design with an awl or chalk on the wrong side of the leather.*

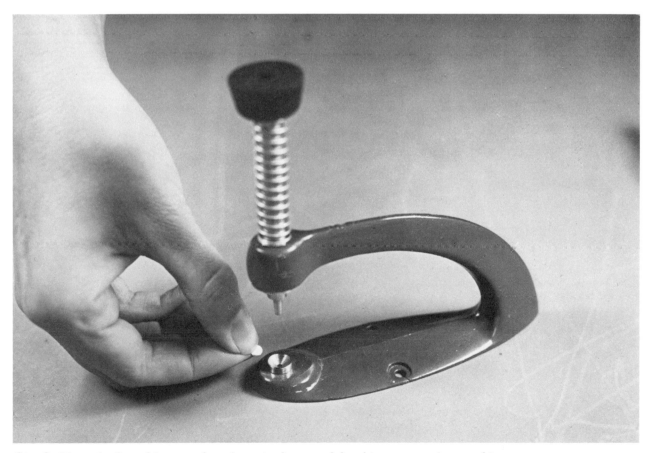

Step 2. *Place the first rhinestone face down in the cup of the rhinestone setting machine.*

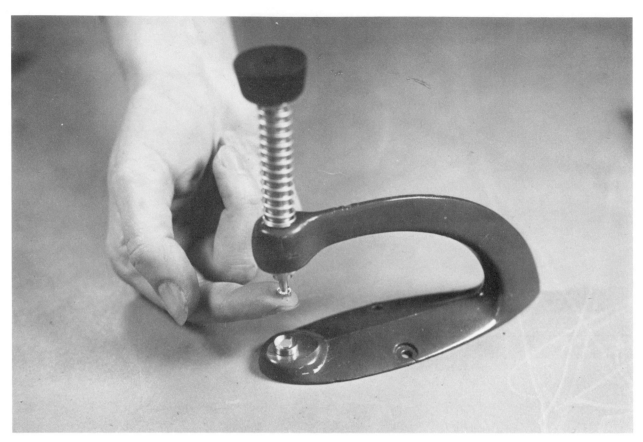

Step 3. *Slip the setting, prongs facing down, onto the upper silver pin.*

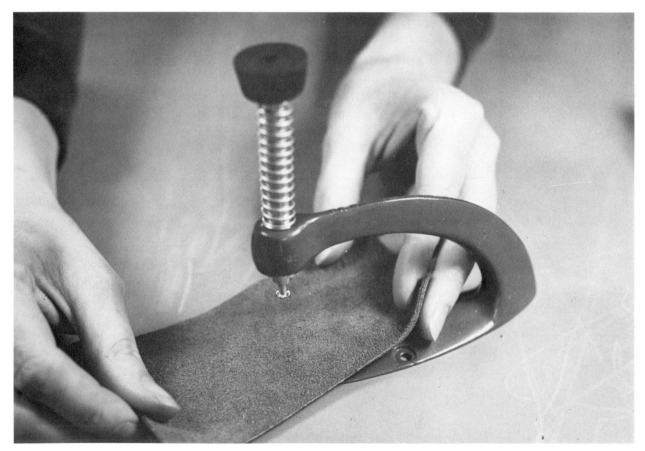

Step 4. *Place the leather over the cup, front side down.*

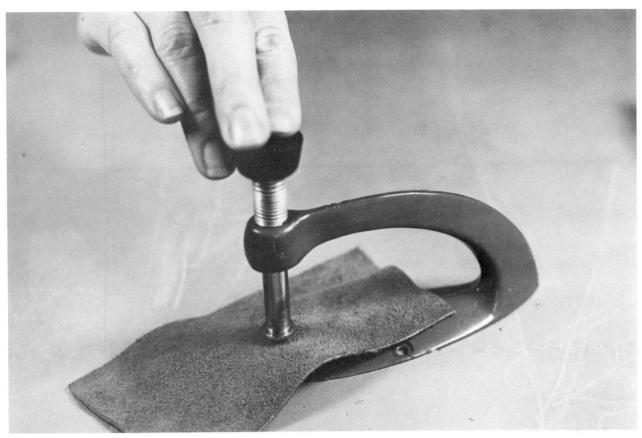

Step 5. *Push down the plunger.*

Step 6. *Continue this process until your rhinestone pattern is complete.*

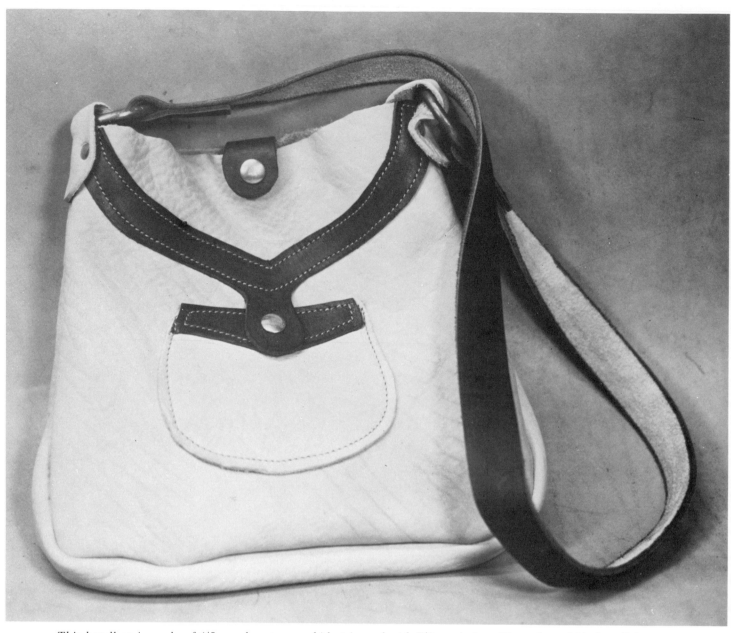

This handbag is made of 4/5 oz. deer tan cowhide trimmed with 7/8 oz. latigo. The soft cowhide is a light golden color and the latigo has been dyed a dark brown for contrast. Note the decorative effect of the front pocket and the two brass snap closings. This bag is machine stitched. By Holy Cow Leather.

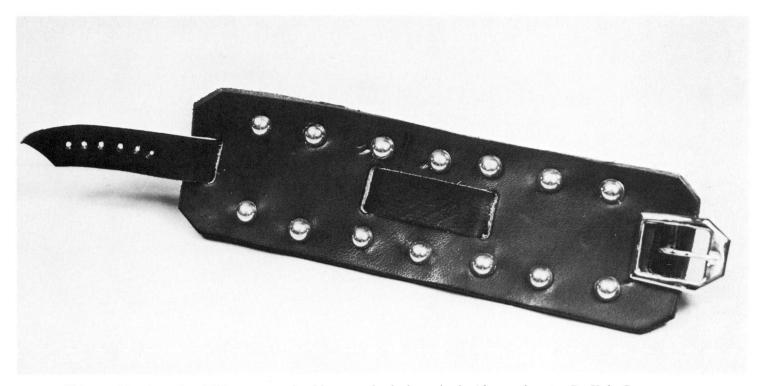

This watchband, made of 6/7 oz. russet shoulder, was dyed, then edged with round spots. By Holy Cow Leather.

15

Hardware

Hardware such as buckles, rings, dees, snaps, and turnlocks of course have a practical use, but their decorative value to a project should also be considered. There are some buckles on the market today which are so elaborate, that the belt becomes a vehicle for showing off the buckle. When choosing a closing for a handbag, you should consider not just which one will be most efficient, but also, which one best suits the style of the bag and will contribute most to its design. In some cases rings, dees, and closings are used when there is no practical purpose for them whatsoever, but are strictly for decoration.

Hardware such as buckles, rings, dees, and dog snaps are attached by inserting a leather strip through them and riveting or stitching it to the project piece. Some turnlocks and clasps are attached by riveting them directly to the leather. Others have prongs which are pushed through the leather and bent over on the back; sometimes these have metal backing plates which help hold the piece in place and protect the leather. The prongs should push through thin leather easily; for heavier leather, start the hole with a small knife slit. If you have difficulty bending the prongs, give them a light tap with a hammer.

MATERIALS

1. Your choice of buckles, rings, dees, dog snaps, turnlocks, and bag clasps.
2. Rawhide mallet.
3. Drawing awl.
4. #1 hole punch and an oblong punch.
5. A chopping block or a 1–2" steel plate.
6. Some heavy scrap leather or rubber.
7. Rivet setter.
8. Rivets.

Choose the hardware to match your leather, that is, use heavy hardware on heavy leather, and more delicate hardware on thinner leather.

PROBLEMS

If you have difficulty putting on buckles with tongues, it could be you're not using a large enough oblong punch. Get a larger one, or use your present tool to overlap the first hole and make it larger.

If the rivets won't go in easily, your rivet holes may be too close to the center bar of the buckle. Lower them a bit. However, if your buckle slides around too much, make your rivet holes closer to the center bar of the buckle.

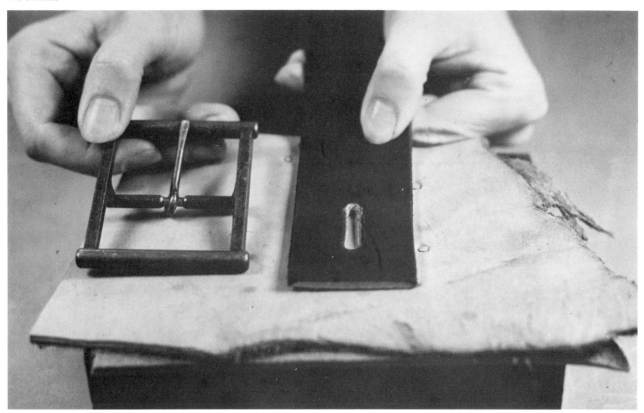

Step 1. *To attach a buckle with a tongue (the movable pin), allow about 2" extra at one end of the belt or strap. Using the oblong or bag punch, make a hole about 3/4" away from the end of the belt. Be certain to make the hole parallel to the sides of the belt and exactly halfway between them. On wide belts, use a 1" or 1-1/2" bag punch; for narrower belts, use a 3/4", 5/8", or 1/2" oblong punch.*

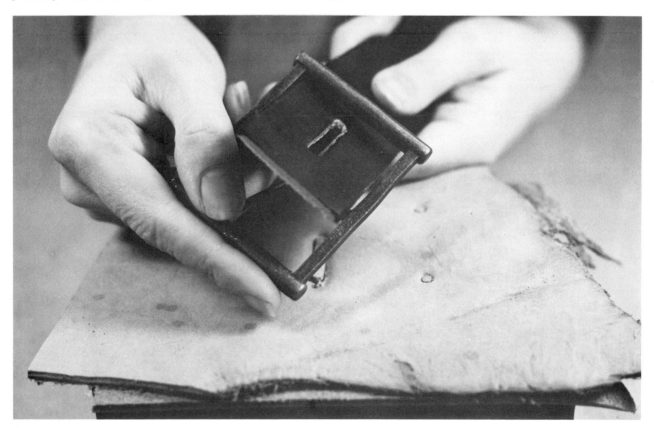

Step 2. *Slide the leather up through the back of the buckle.*

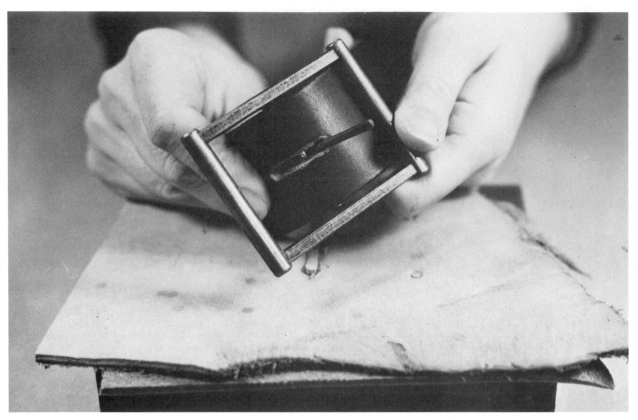

Step 3. *Fit the oblong hole over the tongue and push the end of the leather back down over the center bar.*

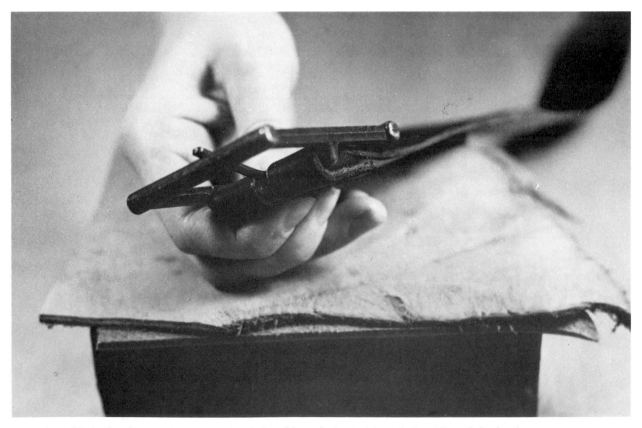

Step 4. *Fold the leather so that the ends of the oblong hole match and the sides of the leather strap are even.*

Step 5. *Punch two holes with the #1 hole punch, one on each side of the tongue, slightly behind it, and centered between the tongue and the edge of the belt. Be careful to punch straight through both pieces of leather.*

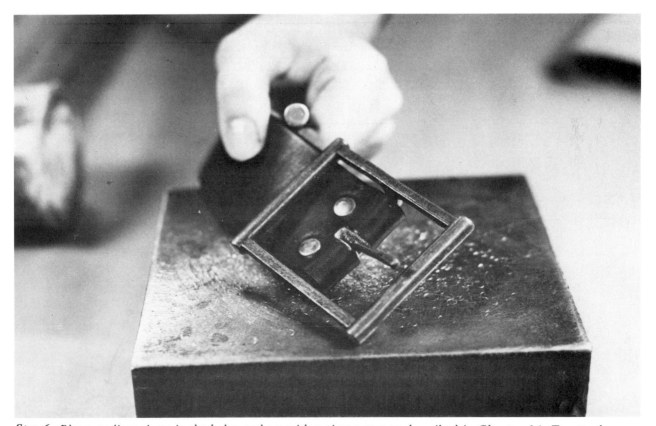

Step 6. *Place medium rivets in the holes and set with a rivet setter as described in Chapter 14. To attach buckles without a tongue, use the same procedure, but eliminate the oblong hole punch.*

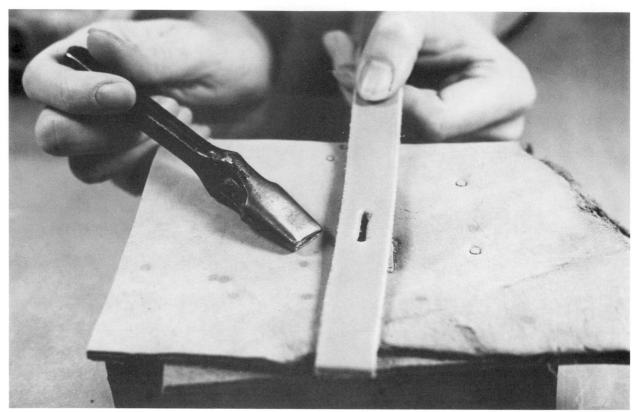

Step 1. *If you're using a harness buckle, you'll have to add a keeper to hold the end of the belt flat against itself. You can either purchase metal keepers, or make leather ones out of thin strips of leather by folding their ends over and riveting or stitching them together. The procedure for attaching a keeper is very simple. Leave an extra 1–2″ at the end of the belt before punching the oblong hole.*

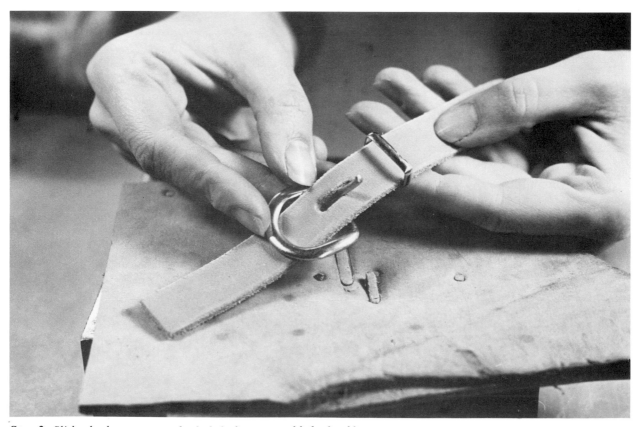

Step 2. *Slide the keeper onto the belt before you add the buckle.*

Step 3. *Rivet the buckle and keeper into place.*

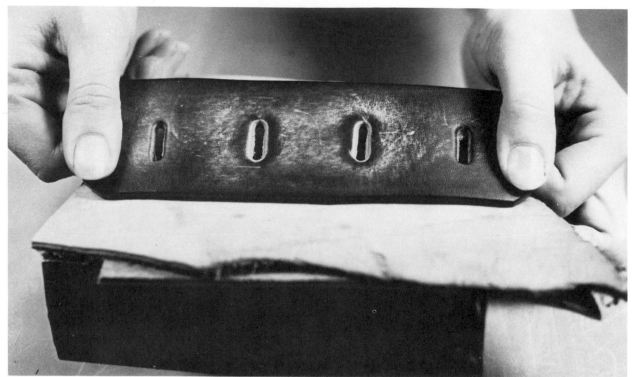

Step 1. *Rings can be woven in and out for a decorative effect on watchbands, wristbands, belts, etc. To do this, you'll need a basic band made from heavy leather, and a narrower strip of thinner leather. (For example, we use 7/8 oz. latigo for the watchband and kip for the strap.) In the heavy leather, punch two oblong holes for each ring, spacing them at intervals equal to the diameter of the ring.*

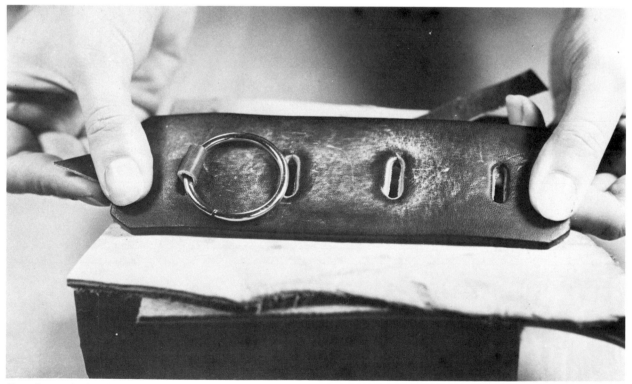

Step 2. *Push the thin strip up through the first hole, over the ring, and back down through the same hole.*

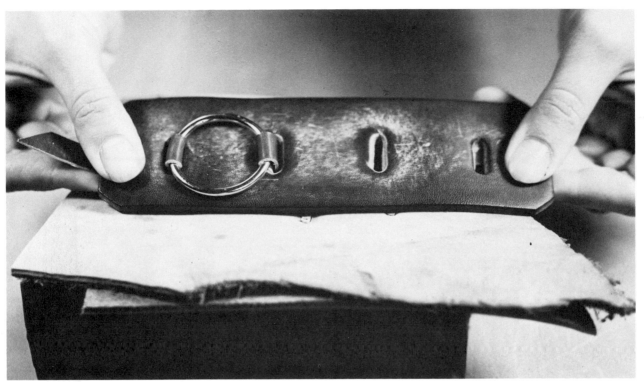

Step 3. *Then push the strip up through the next hole, over the ring, and back down through that hole. Now the ring is held firmly in place.*

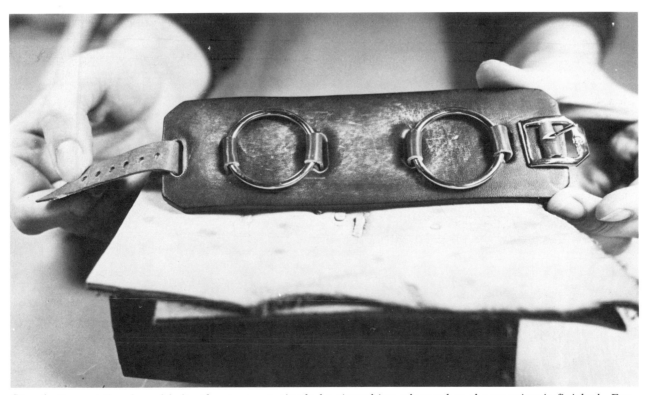

Step 4. *For wristbands and belts, the strap can simply be riveted into place when the weaving is finished. For watchbands, however, a buckle should be added to one end of the strap and holes punched in the other before you begin weaving. An extra oblong hole should be punched about 1/4" from each end of the heavy band, and the thin strap should be pushed down through one of these. At the end of the watchband, the thin strap will come up through the other extra hole and the band will be ready to wear.*

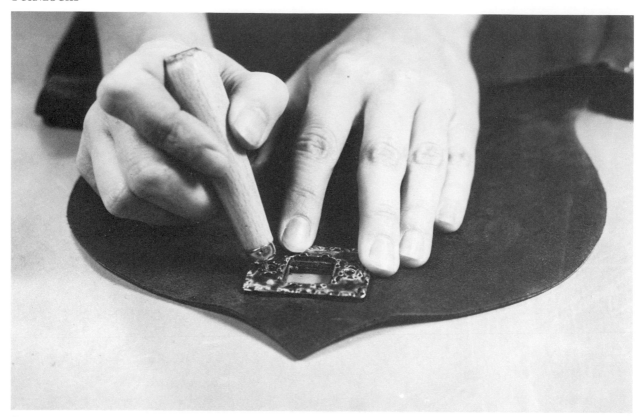

Step 1. *There are many turnlocks and other closings on the market which can be attached with rivets. The hardware comes with holes for just such a purpose. Hold the closing over the leather in the position you want, and mark the holes with an awl.*

Step 2. *Remove the hardware and punch the holes with a #1 hole punch. Use small or medium rivets to attach the hardware.*

This briefcase, made of 6–7 oz. yellow latigo, combines the decorative with the useful: note the straps and buckles. Designed by Becky Stevens, Ithaca, New York.

An attractive strap-and-ring closing was used on this latigo handbag. By Holy Cow Leather.

A front pocket and brass turnlock enhance this handbag. By Holy Cow Leather.

Note the decorative usage of straps and rings on this handbag. By Holy Cow Leather.

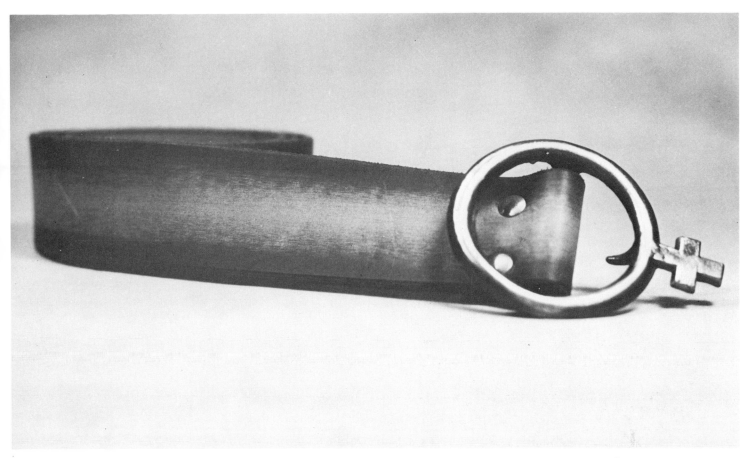

Here, a brass women's symbol buckle is combined with a softly shaded latigo belt. By Lyn Taetzsch.

This 3/4" belt has a gilt buckle and keeper. The design was painted with brush and dye. By Lyn Taetzsch.

These buckles are just a few examples of the wide variety of decorative belt buckles available on the market. The two top left are enamelled brass, from India. The top right is a Britanium pewter steel head. The bottom center, with the mushroom design, is made of leather. The bottom right is stained glass. The two top center are cast brass. By Just Brass Inc.

Suppliers List

Here is a list of suppliers from whom you can obtain all the materials mentioned in the preceding chapters. After you've looked up the suppliers you wish to contact, you'll find their full addresses on page 156. Of course, you should also check out your local art supply shop, fabric and sewing machine store, stationer's, hardware store, shoe repair shop, and scrap steel yard.

Acrylic Paint

Bergen Arts & Crafts

Buckles

Berman Leather Co.
Just Brass, Inc.
Skil-Crafts
Tandy Leather Co.
Trinity Buckle Co.

Closings and Turnlocks

Berman Leather Co.
Mac Leather Co.
M. Siegel Co., Inc.
Skil-Crafts
Tandy Leather Co.

Daubers

Berman Leather Co.
Fiebing Chemical Co.
Mac Leather Co.
Skil-Crafts
Tandy Leather Co.

Dees

Berman Leather Co.
Mac Leather Co.
M. Siegal Co., Inc.
Skil-Crafts
Tandy Leather Co.

Dyes

Berman Leather Co.
Fiebing Chemical Co.
Mac Leather Co., Inc.
Skil-Crafts
Tandy Leather Co.

Harness Dressing

Fiebing Chemical Co.

Heavy Duty Thread

Berman Leather Co.
Ideal Thread Co., Inc.
Tandy Leather Co.

Ink, Markers, and Pens

Bergen Arts & Crafts
Skil-Crafts

Laces

Berman Leather Co.
Tandy Leather Co.

Leather

Berman Leather Co.
Hermann Oak Leather
Mac Leather Co.
M. Siegel Co., Inc.
Tandy Leather Co.

Leather Glue

Tandy Leather Co.

Leather Scissors

Berman Leather Co.
Mac Leather Co.
M. Siegel Co., Inc.
Tandy Leather Co.

Mallets

Berman Leather Co.
Mac Leather Co.
M. Siegel Co., Inc.
Skil-Crafts
Tandy Leather Co.

Paintbrushes

Bergen Arts & Crafts
Skil-Crafts

Rhinestone and Stud Kit

Fashionella

Rings

Berman Leather Co.
Mac Leather Co.
M. Siegel Co., Inc.
Skil-Crafts
Tandy Leather Co.

Rivets, Spots, and Studs

Berman Leather Co.
Mac Leather Co.
M. Siegel Co., Inc.
Skil-Crafts
Tandy Leather Co.

Saddle Soap

Berman Leather Co.
Fiebing Chemical Co.
Mac Leather Co.
M. Siegel Co., Inc.
Tandy Leather Co.

Sheepskin Scraps

Tandy Leather Co.

Stamping Tools

Berman Leather Co.
Mac Leather Co.
Skil-Crafts
Tandy Leather Co.

Stitching Awls

Berman Leather Co.
Mac Leather Co.
M. Siegel Co., Inc.
Skil-Crafts
Tandy Leather Co.

Tooling Sets (Modeling Tools)

Berman Leather Co.
Mac Leather Co.
M. Siegel Co., Inc.
Skil-Crafts
Tandy Leather Co.

Utility Knives

Berman Leather Co.
Mac Leather Co.
M. Siegel Co., Inc.
Skil-Crafts
Tandy Leather Co.

Wing Dividers

Skil-Crafts
Tandy Leather Co.

Wood and Leather Burners

Tandy Leather Co.

Woodcarving Tools

Bergen Arts & Crafts

Addresses

Bergen Arts & Crafts
P.O. Box 381
Marblehead, Massachusetts 01945
catalog $1.00

Berman Leather Co.
145-147 South Street
Boston, Massachusetts 02111
free catalog

Fashionella
P.O. Box 915
Lindhurst, New York 11757

Fiebing Chemical Co.
516 South Second Street
Milwaukee, Wisconsin 53204
wholesale only

Hermann Oak Leather
4050 N. First Street
St. Louis, Missouri 63147

Ideal Thread Co., Inc.
714 Broadway
New York, New York 10003

Just Brass, Inc., a divison of
Richter Bros.
1612 Decatur Street
Ridgewood, New York 11227
catalog $1.00

Mac Leather Co.
424 Broome Street
New York, New York 10013
free catalog

M. Siegel Co., Inc.
186 South Street
Boston, Massachusetts 02111
free catalog

Skil-Crafts, a division of
Brown Leather Co., Inc.
305 Virginia Avenue
P.O. Box 105
Joplin, Missouri 64801
catalog $1.50

Tandy Leather Co.
300 Fifth Avenue
New York, New York 10001
free catalog

Trinity Buckle Co.
P.O. Box 5169
Santa Monica, California 90405
free catalog

British Suppliers

Tools, Fittings, and Buckles

Batchelor
39 Netherhall Gardens
London N.W.3.

Taylor and Company Tools Limited
54 Old Street
London E.C.1.

Skins and Other Supplies

H. Band and Co. Limited
Brent Way
High Street
Brentford
Middlesex

Bevingtons and Sons Limited
166 Abbey Street
London S.E.1.

Burnaby and Chantrell Limited
Liverpool 3
England

Cotswold Leathercraft
Shortwood
Nailsworth
Gloucestershire

J. & W. Dunn Limited
54 Tanner Street
London S.E.1.

J. Hewit and Sons
97 St. John Street
London E.C.1.

R. E. Kohnstamm Limited
Beckenham
Kent

Light Leather Co. Limited
18 Newman Street
London W.1.

Quality First
27 Court Drive
Stanmore
Middlesex

Redpath Campbell & Partners Limited
Cheapside
Strand
Gloucestershire

Index

Edited by Claire Hardiman
Designed by Bob Fillie
Composed in 11 point Times Roman by Gerard Associates/Graphic Arts
All projects by Lyn Taetzsch and Holy Cow Leather were photographed by Herb Genfan.